San Antonio
A CULTURAL TAPESTRY

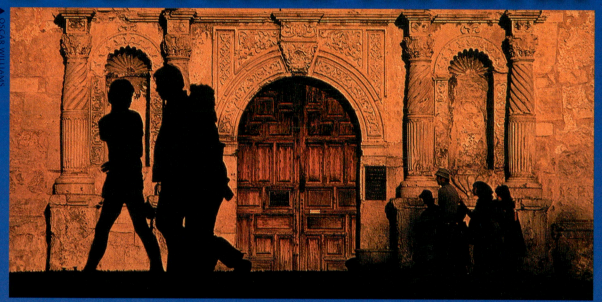
▲ OSCAR WILLIAMS

San Antonio
A CULTURAL TAPESTRY
By Jan Jarboe Russell and Mark Langford

★

**Profiles in Excellence by
Cathy Smith**

★

**Captions by
Patti Larsen**

★

**Art Direction by
Robert Shatzer**

★

**Sponsored by
The Greater San Antonio
Chamber of Commerce**

URBAN TAPESTRY SERIES
TOWERY PUBLISHING, INC.

LIBRARY OF CONGRESS CATALOGING-IN-PUBLICATION DATA
Russell, Jan Jarboe, 1951-
    San Antonio : a cultural tapestry / by Jan Jarboe Russell and Mark Langford ; profiles in excellence by Cathy Smith ; captions by Patti Larsen ; art direction by Robert Shatzer.
       p. cm. — (Urban tapestry series)
  "Sponsored by the Greater San Antonio Chamber of Commerce."
  Includes index.
  ISBN 1-881096-55-6 (alk. paper)
  1. San Antonio (Tex.)—Civilization. 2. San Antonio (Tex.)--Pictorial works. 3. Business enterprises—Texas—San Antonio. 4. San Antonio (Tex.)—Economic conditions. I. Langford, Mark. 1957- . II. Smith, Cathy (Mary Catherine) III. Title. IV. Series.
F394.S2115R87 1998
976.4'351—DC21   98-6742

Copyright ©1998 by Towery Publishing, Inc.

All rights reserved. No part of this work may be reproduced or copied in any form or by any means, except for brief excerpts in conjunction with book reviews, without prior written permission of the publisher.

TOWERY PUBLISHING, INC., 1835 UNION AVENUE, MEMPHIS, TN 38104

PUBLISHER:
J. Robert Towery
EXECUTIVE PUBLISHER:
Jenny McDowell
NATIONAL SALES MANAGER:
Stephen Hung
MARKETING DIRECTOR:
Carol Culpepper
PROJECT DIRECTORS:
Robert Philips, Betsy Schneider, William Brett Sechrest, David Simon, Michele Sylvestro
EXECUTIVE EDITOR:
David B. Dawson
MANAGING EDITOR:
Michael C. James
SENIOR EDITORS:
Lynn Conlee, Carlisle Hacker
EDITORS/PROJECT MANAGERS:
Lori Bond, Jana Files
STAFF EDITORS:
Mary Jane Adams, Susan Hesson, Brian Johnston
ASSISTANT EDITORS:
Rebecca Green, Allison Ring
EDITORIAL CONTRIBUTORS:
Tina Hultgren, Loydean Thomas
CREATIVE DIRECTOR:
Brian Groppe
PROFILE DESIGNERS:
Laurie Beck, Kelley Pratt, Ann Ward
DIGITAL COLOR SUPERVISOR:
Brenda Pattat
DIGITAL COLOR TECHNICIANS:
Jack Griffith, Darin Ipema, Jason Moak, Beverly Timmons
PRODUCTION RESOURCES MANAGER:
Dave Dunlap Jr.
PRODUCTION ASSISTANTS:
Geoffrey Ellis, Enrique Espinosa, Robin McGehee
PRINT COORDINATOR:
Tonda Thomas

Contents

SAN ANTONIO: A CULTURAL TAPESTRY 6
"Though 1 million people live and work here, somehow San Antonio has the feel of a pueblo, a city of houses with red tile roofs built around patios and a downtown of skyscrapers organized around plazas suitable for strolling."

PROFILES IN EXCELLENCE 136
A look at the corporations, businesses, professional groups, and community service organizations that have made this book possible.

PHOTOGRAPHERS 204

INDEX OF PROFILES 206

JAN JARBOE RUSSELL

ONE OF THE OLDEST STORIES TOLD in San Antonio is the legend of La Llorona, the Weeping Woman, who lives on the banks of the San Antonio River and only comes out after 11 p.m. when it is safe to show her face. Even then, she keeps her face covered with a black shawl because, according to many who claim to have seen her, La Llorona has a face both too beautiful and too ugly to behold.

Dora Elizondo Guerra, a librarian who specializes in the English translation of the records of the first Spanish settlers to the city, first heard the story of La Llorona on a hot summer night while seated on her aunt's porch. As Guerra remembers it, her aunt told her that La Llorona was a woman who had once had four beautiful daughters—a daughter for each of the four winds. However, she had been forced to drown her children in the San Antonio River to save them from a fate more terrible than death, the loss of their own souls. Each night, her ghost paces along the river's bank looking for her children. When no one is looking, she uses her shawl as a net to scoop four fish from the river. One by one, the four fish magically transform into her four daughters. The mother and daughters are reunited until, at dawn's first light, La Llorona carefully places each one back into the river, where they spend their days masquerading as fish. "I don't remember not knowing that story," says Guerra. "It gave my life an invisible dimension. The message for me was simple: Life is short. Don't lose your soul."

© DONOVAN REESE

Pure San Antonio: With a Hispanic population nearing 60 percent, the Mexican-American influences on the Fiesta City's rich culture are reflected in its art and architecture, its flavors, and its sounds.

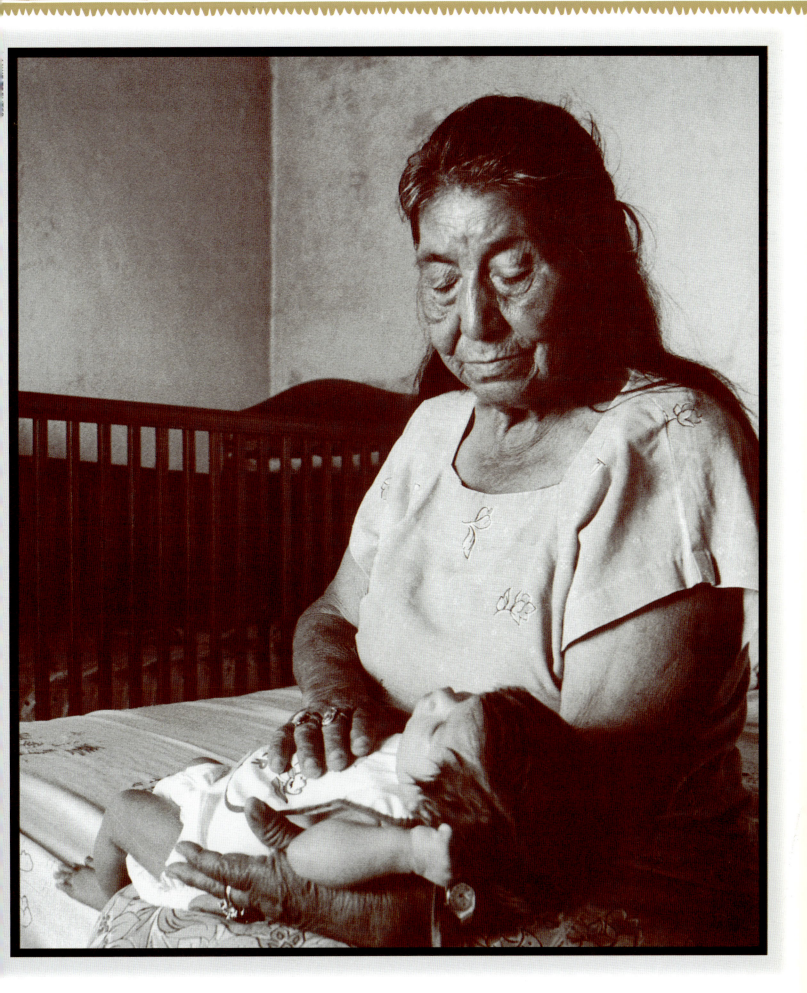

The details and circumstances of La Llorona's story vary from neighborhood to neighborhood, from family to family, from person to person, according to whose grandmother or great-grandmother first told them the story. La Llorona has become part of the city's oral Hispanic history. The central lesson of La Llorona—how to protect the river of life from all kinds of deaths, both spiritual and economic—has become San Antonio's primary soul task. The protagonist, a grief-stricken woman, serves as a mythical conscience for the city. Over the years, many who have embodied her spirit have reminded us that what shapes San Antonio is first and foremost our river, a dark and private world that moves beneath us at all times.

In the midst of our modern endeavors, La Llorona's message permeates our lives with the wisdom of the past: Don't pave over your river, she tells us. Don't allow the five missions built in the 18th century on the river's edge to deteriorate; they remind you of your origins, of a cool, shady outpost on a distant and remote frontier. Put the Alamo on the shiny postcards, but for heaven's sake, keep rethinking the story. It's a good story, a many-layered epic; don't let it go stale. Be what you are, La Llorona advises: a big, boisterous town not far from the border. Tex-Mex and proud of it. A little on edge, like your food and your music.

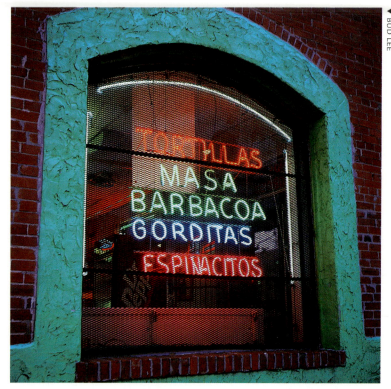

Founded in 1718, long before Texas won its independence from Mexico, San Antonio is one of the oldest cities in the United States. Its traditional Tex-Mex food, music, and dress are constant reminders of an earlier time.

Elegant Victorian homes and buildings line the streets of the King William Historic District, which lies just a few blocks south of downtown.

In all likelihood, the story originated in the early 1500s when Spanish conquistadores invaded the Aztecs in Mexico. San Antonio was once a part of Mexico. Fifty-eight percent of the people who live here now are Mexican-American.

And cities, like people, are formed by the stories they tell, as much as they are formed by the laying of brick or the mixing of mud and water. The telling of legends—like that of La Llorona—is part of the reason why out-of-town visitors who come here

instantly find San Antonio so charming and picturesque. At a feeling level, they recognize that even though San Antonio is the eighth-largest city in the United States, it still has the innocence of a small village. Though 1 million people live and work here, somehow San Antonio has the feel of a pueblo, a city of houses with red tile roofs built around patios and a downtown of sky-scrapers organized around plazas suitable for strolling.

A CULTURAL TAPESTRY

THE SECRET OF SAN ANTONIO IS SIMPLY this: We are a real place, but we haven't yet given our magic away. The legend of La Llorona is one way we store magic. Those who have grown up with variations of this legend—and, hence, with this magic—are affected on many levels, not all of them metaphorical or symbolic. The story shaped the life of Dr. Julian Trevino, a college professor and vice president of the San Antonio Independent School District, who heard it from his grandmother, Josefina. Trevino says the story has helped him stay true to his family's dreams: He stayed put in San Antonio, where he now has primary responsibility for managing students from the inner city, trying to keep them from selling themselves down the river of poverty and urban violence.

Trevino's mother, Maria, who immigrated to San Antonio from Mexico in 1916, was also strongly influenced by the La Llorona legend. It is no accident that, each week, Mrs. Trevino, the owner of a  popular restaurant called El Mirador, provides the real chicken soup that feeds San Antonio's soul. Every Saturday morning, the line starts forming early outside El Mirador, a small stucco restaurant with seats for only 130 customers. From all four quadrants of the city, San Antonians of all races, classes, and ages converge upon the restaurant for their weekly $4.95 bowl of sopa azteca, a Mexican soup made of chicken, tomatoes, garlic, spinach, cheese, and secret herbs known only to Mrs. Trevino. "A little *epazote* [Mexican tea], a little *comino* [cumin] . . . you know, this and that, cooked over a slow grill, then blended all together in a crazy stew," explains Mrs. Trevino, laughing now, "just like life." In the cauldrons where her soup comes to life, there lives the spirit of La Llorona.

MIKE TREUTER

"Let's meet at El Mirador!" has become a legendary Saturday morning invitation—after which deals have been made, friendships forged, and political careers launched over steaming bowls of the restaurant's famous sopa azteca. Dr. Julian Trevino, vice president of the city's public school district, and his mother, Maria, owner of El Mirador, are justifiably proud of the role they continue to play in fostering their family's dream, as well as a true San Antonio tradition.

A Cultural Tapestry

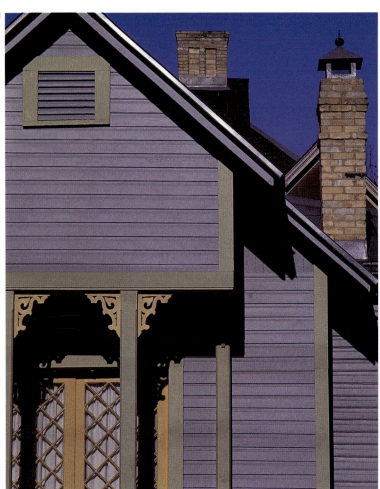

The historic heart of San Antonio is La Villita—the little village—built in the late 1700s as one of the city's original Spanish settlements. Today, restored buildings house shops, galleries, and restaurants, all nestled among high-rise luxury hotels and office towers.

This soup in turn became the basis of a citywide ritual. O'Neil Ford, San Antonio's premier architect, began showing up at El Mirador with artists, friends, and writers, who joined the working-class people from the neighborhood who were already El Mirador's regulars. In no time, the parking lot was full of Mercedes, BMWs, and Range Rovers, as well as the pickup trucks, family vans, and Fords that had been there first.

In a corner booth, Ford would hold forth about the fate of the city, often gesturing wildly with an unlit cigar in one hand and a wet soup spoon in the other. "I hate whimsy," I remember him saying one particular Saturday morning. "Buildings, like this soup, need to be simply made from good, authentic ingredients by imaginative people who know how all the parts go together."

It was Ford who, more than any other single individual, made modern-day San Antonio look like San Antonio. He moved to town from Dallas in 1938 in order to restore La Villita, the original settlement for the Spanish soldiers and families who were

ZINTGRAFF COLLECTION, THE INSTITUTE OF TEXAN CULTURES, SAN ANTONIO, TEXAS

stationed at the Alamo in the early 1800s. By the time Ford arrived more than a hundred years later, La Villita was a slum.

Many of the people in charge at City Hall and other places wanted to tear down all the old houses and rebuild something horrible and modern called Ye Olde Spanish Village. Somehow, Ford prevailed (he was, after all, Irish, and not without his own magic) and restored La Villita to its original design. First, he shored up the old houses using native stone and indigenous materials, and then he grouped them around a series of small plazas, working from drawings made by Spanish priests in the 1700s. Once renovated, La Villita became the public face of modern San Antonio, one that reflected the materials and values that Ford cared most about: history, stone, shade, quiet design, and the firm rejection of all pretense.

Using these same principles, Ford went on to restore most of what we now see in San Antonio. He restored San Fernando Cathedral, and designed and built all of HemisFair Park, site of

Considered the beginning of the city's modern-day tourist industry, HemisFair '68 transformed 92 acres of downtown property into an international exposition (RIGHT). More recent downtown developments include the Paseo del Alamo, a terraced stream and water garden that connects the River Walk and Alamo Plaza (LEFT).

A CULTURAL TAPESTRY 15

the World's Fair in 1968, including the Tower of the Americas, the steel needle that still dominates the city's skyline. In a small hillside just north of downtown, Ford chiseled a massive collection of buildings that form Trinity University. Before he died in July 1982, he designed and built the walkway that links the city's two most important features, the San Antonio River and the Alamo. I remember a conversation with Ford as he stood on the river's side of Alamo Plaza as the walkway was being constructed. He explained that in his mind's eye, he envisioned the walkway as a way to tell the story of San Antonio's water supply: Out of stone, he built a sculpture to represent the underground springs that feed the San Antonio River; then he built a series of small ditches that transport water. The ditches, cascading from the Alamo to the river's edge, remind us of how the city's water was first put to practical use in 1718. That's when eight engineered *acequias* (hand-dug ditches) were designed by Spanish priests and built by Indians. For nearly 200 years, the *acequias* have diverted water from the river, opening up land for farming, for pastures, and later for all the industries that support the city, including tourism and the military. "What I wanted to do was put the Alamo in the proper context," Ford told me. "Without the river, there wouldn't have been an Alamo. Instead of 'Remember the Alamo,' the slogan for San Antonio should be 'Remember the River.'"

OSCAR WILLIAMS

Canary Islanders came to the area in 1731 and laid the cornerstone of the original San Fernando Cathedral seven years later. The walls of that first church form the altar area of the present-day Gothic Revival sanctuary, completed in 1873. The oldest cathedral in the United States, San Fernando is the home parish for many San Antonians, some of whom trace their ancestry to the city's original settlers.

ORD DID NOT LEARN THAT LESSON ON his own. He had been inspired as a young man by a group of women artists, who in 1924 put on "The Goose That Laid the Golden Egg," a puppet show that gave rise to the San Antonio Conservation Society. One of the issues that galvanized the women was a proposal in 1921 to pave over the San Antonio River with concrete for use as a flood control channel. Early that spring, a flood had forced the river to overflow its banks, causing millions of dollars in damage and taking the lives of 50 people. At that time, San Antonio was enjoying a boom: It was the largest city in Texas, with more skyscrapers than Dallas. The city commissioners viewed the flood-prone river as a threat to prosperity. It was a defining moment for the city, and into it stepped Emily Edwards, an artist and former high school drama teacher, acting as yet another La Llorona protagonist.

The puppet show lasted only 10 minutes. In it, Edwards urged city commissioners not to kill the very things that fed San Antonio's authentic prosperity. She and her friends made puppets out of cloth with black button eyes. The story was about an imaginary couple, named Mr. and Mrs. San Antonio, who quarreled over the fate of a goose, symbolizing the soul of the city. Mr. San Antonio wanted to kill the goose immediately to get all the gold, while Mrs. San Antonio argued that if the goose were spared, she would lay more eggs. The heroine of the story held a basket with five golden eggs labeled as follows: Heart of Texas, Missions, History, Tourists, and Beauty. Mr. San Antonio complained about the goose's inefficiency. "She waddles and she winds when she swims on the river," he said. But Mrs. San Antonio persisted: "Her home is old buildings that won't fall down, and she keeps us from looking just like every other town."

© DONOVAN REESE

San Antonio has retained its charm over the years by upholding such traditions as the hand-painted eggshell *cascarónes*. Still sold by the dozens during Fiesta, these confetti-filled novelties are playfully cracked on the heads of both unsuspecting friends and willing participants. Inspiring a similar reverence for the past is the San Antonio Conservation Society, which makes its home in the Anton Wulff House. Located in the King William Historic District, this architectural gem was built in 1878 by Anton Frederick Wulff, landscaper of Alamo Plaza.

Located on a graceful bend in the San Antonio River, the Arneson River Theatre offers year-round musical entertainment, from mariachi and country and western to pop and opera.

The goose was allowed to live, and history has long since vindicated Mrs. San Antonio. Instead of paving over the river, a horseshoe-shaped channel was built along the downtown portion of the river to control its flow. Now the bend known as the River Walk is the city's number one tourist attraction. Every night of the year, thousands of visitors move down the banks of the river conga-style, traveling from restaurant to restaurant, shop to shop, leaving behind their gold. With the opening of Planet Hollywood and the Hard Rock Cafe in recent years, some natives became concerned that the River Walk was beginning to

look like an underground mall. But the basic design of the River Walk—an urban ribbon of shops that threads beneath bridges and arches, the most romantic urban park in America—remains intact. In the future, it will be home to Planet Internet, or whatever new trend happens to surface.

    Besides, it is still possible as well to find authentic San Antonio gems among all the neon. For instance, Jim Cullum's jazz band plays nightly at the Hyatt Regency Hotel, and there's nothing homogenized about the bright yellow nachos at the Esquire Bar, to say nothing of the bottled beer.

In 1958, the Greater San Antonio Chamber of Commerce began studies on river development that ultimately led to the Paseo del Río project, which today features approximately three miles of hotels, restaurants, clubs, shops, galleries, and outdoor cafés lining both sides of the San Antonio River.

Barges operated by Yanaguana Cruises make their way up and down the river, providing narrated tours of one of Texas' top attractions.

ON THE STREET LEVEL, IT IS POSSIBLE to see some of what stirs San Antonio out of its watery deep. There is the Alamo, of course, site of the famous, bloody battle between Texas settlers and the Mexican army in 1836. If Texas were a religion, not just a state, then the Alamo would be the holy of holies. Even though the Texans lost the battle of the Alamo, they went on to win the land we call Texas a few weeks later at the Battle of San Jacinto.

These days, the Alamo means different things to different people. To some, it symbolizes the last stand—a place where William Travis, the very first Texan, fought and died for the right to a second chance. This has become the embodiment of the great Texas myth, the idea of starting again—of striking it rich, if not this year, then maybe next. To many, however, the Alamo is a symbol of conquest. The Texans were fighting for land that belonged to Mexico. It was a war over real estate, and ultimately the Mexicans lost. In a city with the largest percent of Mexican-Americans in the United States, it's easy to understand why the Alamo carries equal measures of guilt and heroism.

◀ OSCAR WILLIAMS Built in 1718 as the city's first mission, the Alamo remains a symbol of the independent spirit that makes Texas unique. In 1836, some 180 brave souls defended the fort against Mexican General Antonio López de Santa Anna and his army of thousands. Although all of the hometown troops lost their lives in the 13-day siege, the famous battle cry "Remember the Alamo" sparked the defeat of the Mexican army at San Jacinto a month later. Marking the 100th anniversary of the historic conflict, a marble cenotaph was erected on Alamo Plaza in 1936 to commemorate the defenders, whose names are chiseled into its base.

A Cultural Tapestry

The truth is always dim, and can only be discovered by going farther back in time. The battle that fixed our history only lasted 13 days. There is an older, just-as-true history to the Alamo, one that foreshadows life in modern-day San Antonio. Before it was a battlefield, the Alamo was a mission—an odd mixture of Mexican, American, and Indian styles that all came together because of the easy access to the river. And that powerful attraction still exists today. "I've never been to the Alamo," explains El Mirador's Maria Trevino. "But I don't have anything against it. It just means we get the best of both worlds. To me, Mexico is like a grandmother. I like to remember her from time to time, but this is my country. This is the place that gives me my bread and butter."

Even in modern San Antonio, it's not difficult to find evidence of La Llorona still at work shaping the city. To find her in her most instinctive element, though, it is necessary to follow the San Antonio River south for two, maybe three miles, where there are few tourists and the river is still wild. Just behind Mission San Juan Capistrano, there is a mile-long nature walk, where

it is still possible to see the river as it was hundreds of years ago. Often, the river is muddy and brown, because it is carrying a heavy load of debris from the north. In some places, there are pools of stagnant water where the only visible signs of life are minnows and an occasional dragonfly. Often, however, you will see white herons, their scrawny legs miraculously holding up magnificent wings, landing and taking off on the river's edge. Snakes slither, too. From here, you can plainly see how the river runs, how it picks up everything—sticks and stones and all of the other things that make up the city's life—holds it for just a little while, and then carries everything in its slow, strong current out to sea.

One of the hallmarks of San Antonio is its rich link to the past. Tourists and locals alike treasure both century-old Alamo artifacts and the beautiful Paseo del Río.

San Antonio boasts one of the shortest drive times from the airport to the central business district (approximately 14 minutes) of any major metropolitan area in the United States. Serving as a structural beacon for those on their way into the city is the Tower Life Building, which at one time was the tallest skyscraper in Texas.

The old and the new find common ground in San Antonio, as seen in the parish church of Our Lady of Guadalupe on the city's west side in Guadalupe Plaza (OPPOSITE), and on the San Antonio College campus, with its blend of both modern and historic architecture (LEFT).

A CULTURAL TAPESTRY

An age of elegance is reflected in the details of some of San Antonio's most prominent buildings, from the ornate facade of City Hall (OPPOSITE) to the Bexar County Courthouse, rising in the distance (LEFT). Built in 1892 by the architectural firm of J. Riely Gordon & Laub, the granite courthouse is listed on the National Register of Historic Places.

A CULTURAL TAPESTRY

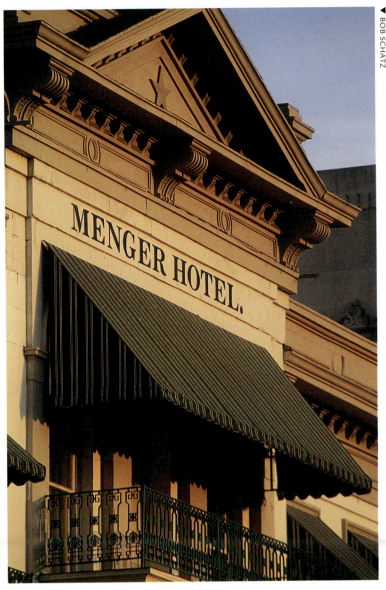

Preserved facades and eye-catching ornamentation are the stars of some of San Antonio's most memorable buildings. Opened in 1859, the Menger Hotel is truly a national landmark (LEFT): Teddy Roosevelt recruited his famous Rough Riders at the Menger Bar, and luminaries such as Sarah Bernhardt and Oscar Wilde have visited its halls. The hotel, which boasts 350 modern rooms, was completely restored in 1989 in celebration of its 130th anniversary.

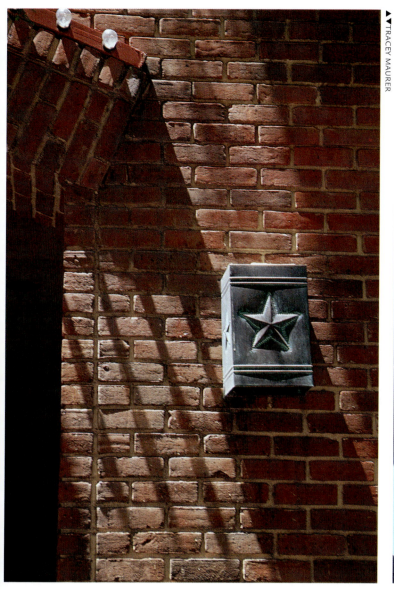

TRACEY MAURER

A CULTURAL TAPESTRY

35

T he art of Mexico adorns the local landscape with colorful charm. Over the years, immigrants arriving from Saltillo, Monterrey, and Mexico City have brought with them a palette of colors that is incorporated into many of San Antonio's hand-painted facades.

A feast for the eyes awaits visitors to downtown San Antonio, where an upward glance often reveals the intricate ornamentation of the past. A bit more refined, but no less impressive, is the Ramada Emily Morgan (OPPOSITE). Completed in the 1920s as the Medical Arts Building and converted to a hotel in 1985, this Gothic Revival structure was one of the first skyscrapers west of the Mississippi.

A CULTURAL TAPESTRY

San Antonio is enriched by the vivid colors of mosaic tiles and painted murals adorning many of its buildings. Especially noteworthy is the winged caretaker watching over the city from Santa Rosa Hospital (OPPOSITE).

Crafted over the years by the pioneers, missionaries, Indians, Spanish and Mexican settlers, and modern visionaries who have made the city unique, San Antonio's diverse decorative elements also include a touch of Greek mythology, as in this sculptural representation of Nike, the goddess of victory (OPPOSITE).

A CULTURAL TAPESTRY

S A N A N T O N I O

Sponsored by the Mexican Ministry of Foreign Affairs, the Mexican Cultural Institute in HemisFair Park offers a look at some of the art and artifacts that characterize San Antonio today and throughout its history.

A CULTURAL TAPESTRY

45

The hotels, museums, and other buildings that form San Antonio's arts and cultural district reflect the old and the new, from gleaming, multistory structures to renovated breweries and warehouses. Each tells a story, different in flavor, but consistent with the city's distinctive ambience.

OSCAR WILLIAMS

CHARLENE FARIS / HILLSTROM STOCK PHOTO

A Cultural Tapestry

Lovers of fine art, beautiful flowers, and intriguing architecture find it all at the Marion Koogler McNay Art Museum (BOTTOM AND OPPOSITE BOTTOM). Set on 25 acres high on a hill in north-central San Antonio, the McNay is considered one of the finest art museums in the United States.

Offering an intriguing setting of its own, the Southwest Craft Center, nestled in a river bend just north of downtown, houses classrooms for weaving, photography, pottery, and other crafts (TOP AND OPPOSITE TOP). The facility—the city's only remaining example of French Provincial architecture—served as the Ursuline Convent and Academy for Girls from 1851 to 1965, when the prime riverfront property was restored by the San Antonio Conservation Society and other groups.

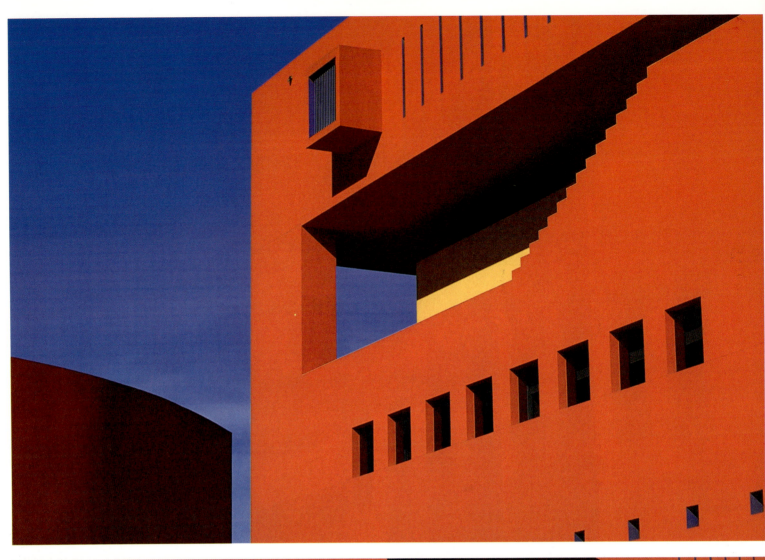

San Antonio

A new color—enchilada red—found its way into the local lexicon with the opening of the striking, 240,000-square-foot main branch of the San Antonio Public Library in May 1995. Although the original library was constructed in the early 1900s from a $50,000 contribution by Andrew Carnegie, it took a $28 million bond issue to help finance the current state-of-the-art facility.

A Cultural Tapestry

SAN ANTONIO

History and education converge at San Antonio's institutions of higher learning. Towers, spires, angels, and other elements signal the rich religious traditions of three local private schools—Our Lady of the Lake University (OPPOSITE TOP), the University of the Incarnate Word (TOP), and Trinity University (BOTTOM). From its new downtown campus, the University of Texas at San Antonio (OPPOSITE BOTTOM) lends a modern twist to the concept of building as sculpture.

A CULTURAL TAPESTRY

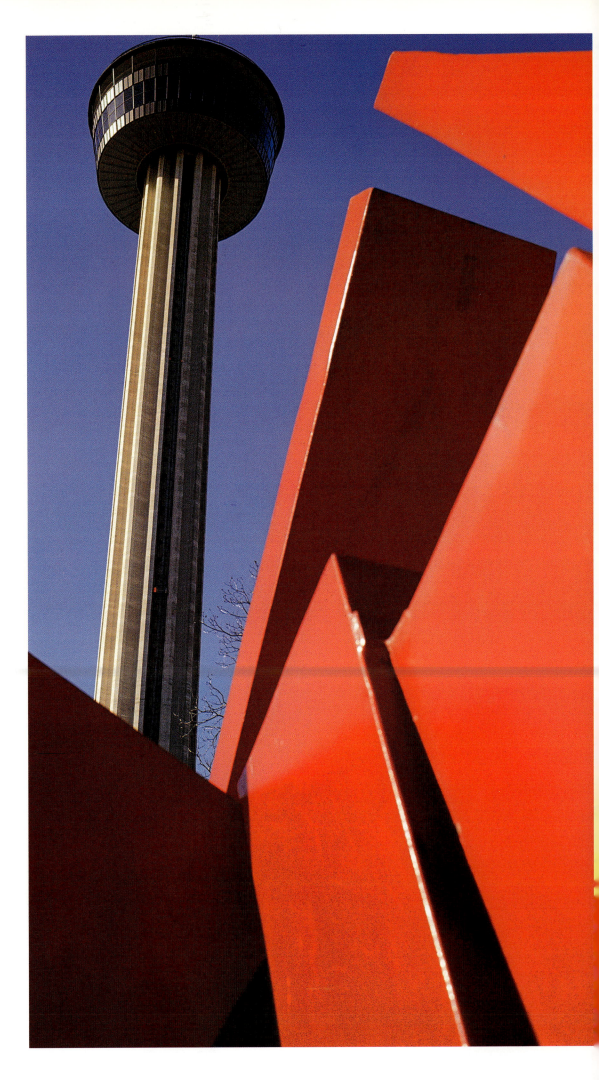

54

SAN ANTONIO

Piercing the sky at 750 feet, the Tower of the Americas (OPPOSITE) was built by local architect O'Neil Ford as the focal point of HemisFair '68. A revolving restaurant greets diners and sightseers who make the trip to the top in a glass-faced elevator. Described by the *New York Times* as "the region's most imaginative architect," Ford designed another well-known tower that graces the campus of Trinity University (LEFT). Standing tall alongside it is *Large Interior Form*, a 16-foot-high bronze piece by renowned British sculptor Henry Moore.

A CULTURAL TAPESTRY

Elegant arches, interesting rooflines, and columns of every variety help give the King William Historic District its unmistakable flair. Small cottages are nestled among mansions—all with architectural styles that run the gamut from Victorian and Italianate to Greek and Gothic Revival to Romanesque and neoclassic. The area was originally settled in the late 19th century by wealthy German families, and its main street was named King William after Kaiser Wilhelm of Prussia.

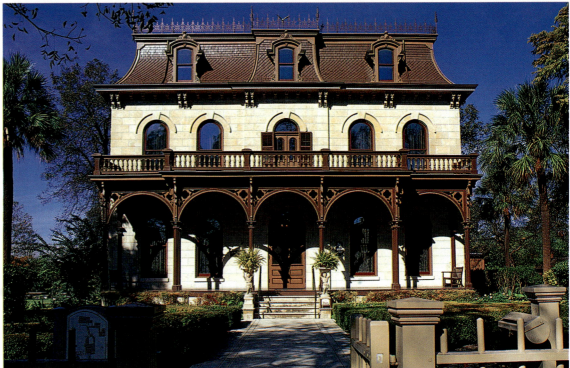

San Antonio

San Antonio's Spanish architectural style carries over into the area's newest neighborhoods and attractions, including the Club at Sonterra. Its golf course, designed by Bruce Devlin and Robert von Hagge, presents water obstacles at nearly every hole, although some golfers might find even greater challenges dodging their FOOORRREE-legged competition.

A CULTURAL TAPESTRY

Located just west of downtown, the Nelson W. Wolff Municipal Stadium is named after one of the city's most popular mayors. Home to baseball's Class AA San Antonio Missions (a Dodger farm team and a member of the Texas League) the stadium seats 8,000 screaming fans—6,000 in the bleachers and 2,000 on the grassy berms.

The passion for roundball can start early in San Antonio, where legions of youngsters hone their skills, some in hopes of making it to the professional ranks. But whatever the level of ability, sports fans of all ages find a place in their hearts for the hometown Spurs. Formed in 1973 as members of the old American Basketball Association, the team joined the NBA in 1976 and has since won nine division titles. Spurs players have appeared in 20 NBA All-Star Games and today are led by David Robinson (OPPOSITE).

A CULTURAL TAPESTRY

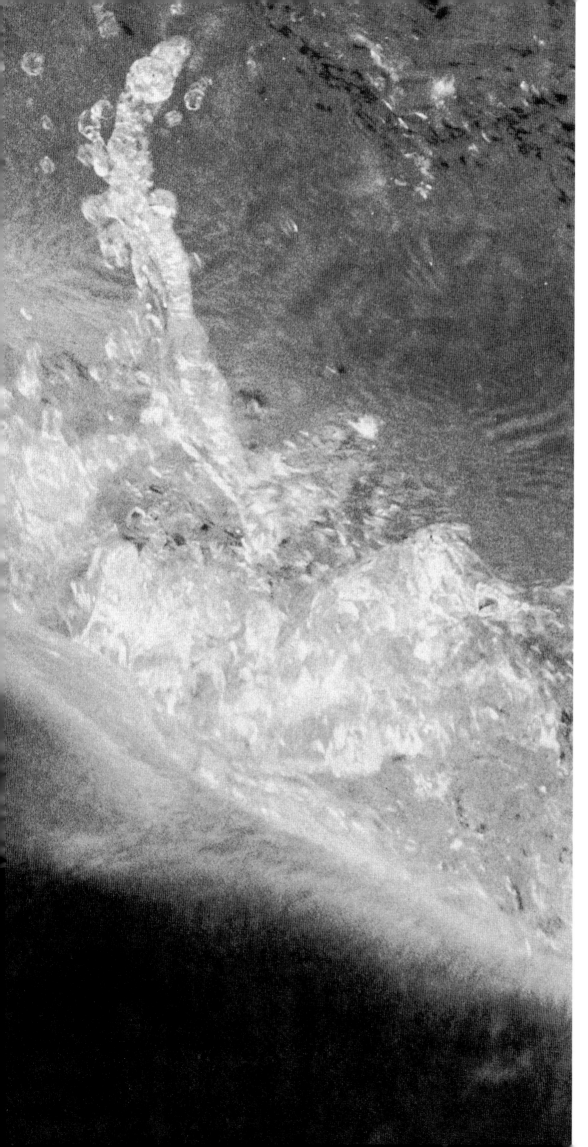

Swimming competitively for more than a decade, San Antonio native Josh Davis thrilled local crowds when he won three gold medals—more than any other man in the U.S. delegation—during the 1996 Olympic Games in Atlanta.

With HemisFair '68, the face of San Antonio changed forever, and tourism rapidly became one of the city's top industries. Continuing that momentum, a public/private partnership extended the San Antonio River and created Rivercenter Mall, with its 1,000-room Marriott Rivercenter hotel that features a one-acre ballroom (LEFT). By 1993, ongoing development had sparked the construction of the Alamodome, a state-of-the-art, multipurpose facility designed to accommodate large annual conventions and trade shows, concerts, religious conferences, and major sporting events, such as the NBA All-Star Game and the NCAA Final Four (OPPOSITE).

A CULTURAL TAPESTRY

Bisected by the beautiful San Antonio River, the city celebrates its aquatic ties through the numerous fountains gracing its buildings and public areas.

Visitors and San Antonians alike can see the city from the river's point of view courtesy of Yanaguana Cruises. In under an hour, boat tours shuttle passengers along a two-mile stretch of the famed Paseo del Río.

A CULTURAL TAPESTRY

Whether man-made or natural, the colors that brighten San Antonio's River Walk can't help but reflect the festive atmosphere created by the area's cafés, camaraderie, and casual fun.

MARK LANGFORD

San Antonians call it Fiesta, and it began in 1891 to commemorate San Jacinto Day. On April 21, 1836, Sam Houston and the Texan Army defeated General Santa Anna's troops and drove them back into Mexico, marking the birth of Texas—and a new nation.

Today, during Fiesta's 10-day celebration of independence and cultural diversity, city streets are alive with dancers, crafts, food, and festivity. Half a million people take in the brightly colored floats, costumes, and bands at the century-old Battle of Flowers Parade (PAGES 74 AND 75).

OSCAR WILLIAMS

MARK LANGFORD

SAN ANTONIO

Rivaled only by Mardi Gras in New Orleans, Fiesta is one of the largest citywide events in the United States. Coinciding with the blooming of wildflowers each spring, the celebration inspires a new attitude amid all the fun and merriment.

A CULTURAL TAPESTRY

The River Parade, held on the first Monday of Fiesta, features the crowning of not one, but two kings. The event is staged annually by the Texas Cavaliers, whose mission is to foster good relations between civilians and the military. A King Antonio is chosen in honor of the city's patron saint, Anthony of Padua, while a second king, El Rey Feo—the Ugly King—is selected by the league of United Latin American Citizens.

A CULTURAL TAPESTRY

Palm Sunday parishioners represent San Antonio's deep religious roots, which include the city's historic Franciscan missions, now open to tourists and worshipers alike.

BOB SCHATZ

SAN ANTONIO

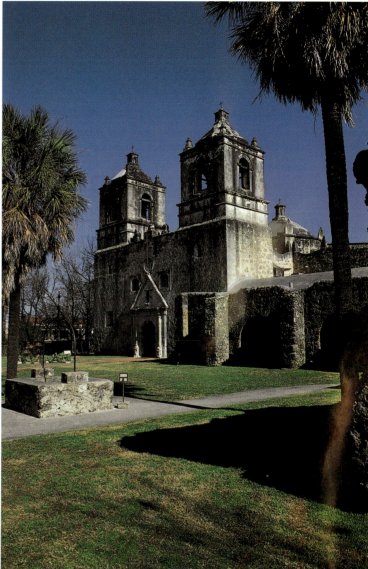

D. CLARKE EVANS

The founding of San Antonio occurred in 1718 when Father Antonio Olivares established Mission San Antonio de Valero, later know as the Alamo. Today, the four missions that followed are run by the Archdiocese of San Antonio in conjunction with the National Park Service. Of the group, San José (LEFT) is the oldest, established in 1720. Concepción (RIGHT), San Juan Capistrano (OPPOSITE RIGHT), and San Francisco de la Espada (OPPOSITE LEFT) all were moved from their original sites in East Texas to their present locations in 1731.

SAN ANTONIO

M aterials used by the settlers to construct San Antonio's missions were those found close at hand—limestone quarried from Brackenridge Park; tufa, a soft rock that is easy to work with; sandstone; and shale. A 5.5-mile trail that originates at Mission Concepción is the departure point for tours of the historic sites.

The Alamo, the Cradle of Texas Liberty, is best known as the site of a bloody battle that ended on March 6, 1836, when all the defenders—among them heroes Davy Crockett and Jim Bowie—were killed and their bodies burned. Visitors to San Antonio are often surprised to find that the Alamo is located literally in the heart of downtown.

Both shrine and museum, the Alamo contains exhibits detailing the battle for Texas independence that was hard fought in San Antonio. In the annual pilgrimage to the Alamo, sponsored by the Daughters of the Republic of Texas, the names of those who lost their lives defending the fortress are intoned as a silent procession of school groups, organizations, businesses, and the military file past, placing commemorative wreaths in front of the historic facade.

MARK LANGFORD

With the history of the Alamo as its backdrop, San Antonio has long been known as a military community. Fort Sam Houston—headquarters of the Fifth U.S. Army and home to Brooke Army Medical Center and the U.S. Army Medical Command—was built in 1876. In the years leading up to World War II, four additional bases were constructed—Kelly, Brooks, Randolph, and Lackland—making the military the city's largest employer.

TOMMY HULTGREN

Prior to its closure in 1995, Kelly Air Force Base was the largest aircraft maintenance facility in the air force (PAGES 92 AND 93), working on the massive C-5 plane, which also served to provide much-needed shade during the many air shows held annually at the base. Today, Kelly is embracing civilian life as it moves toward commercialization with Boeing and other major national and international companies.

With its many historic and educational attractions, Fiesta City is prime territory for both local and vacationing families. The gates of the Witte Museum, which echo the architectural feel of the city, have proven to be a welcoming sight for visitors, especially since the 1997 opening of the HEB Science Treehouse. The four-level, 15,000-square-foot addition appeals to aspiring scientists of all ages from its location behind the museum on the banks of the San Antonio River.

Since it opened in 1995, the San Antonio Children's Museum has been a place for exploring local sites in miniature through exhibits such as Citystreets, Runway #9, and Mission Courtyard. In addition to educational classes in the summer, the kids can go eye-to-eye year-round with the "fishies" in the museum's aquarium.

A Cultural Tapestry

San Antonio

Trading on the area's temperate climate, outdoor enthusiasts can enjoy a variety of wet and wild activities, from tubing on the nearby Comal River (OPPOSITE) to spending a cool afternoon at Splashtown, San Antonio's 15-acre water recreation park (LEFT).

The German village of Spassburg, the 1920s boomtown known as Crackaxle Canyon, and a Mexican villa called Los Festivales are all part of Six Flags Fiesta Texas (TOP AND OPPOSITE TOP). Perhaps better known as home to The Rattler—the world's tallest wooden roller coaster at 179 feet—the park also features the world's only backwards coaster, aptly named The Joker, after the dastardly antagonist of Batman fame.

Another source for a full day of family fun is Brackenridge Park (BOTTOM AND OPPOSITE BOTTOM). Opened in 1899, this mid-city oasis now covers approximately 343 downtown acres and includes among its many offerings a cable-car sky ride. The San Antonio Zoo is also tucked into the park's lush landscape.

A CULTURAL TAPESTRY

SAN ANTONIO

A leader in marine research and conservation, Sea World of Texas blends education with a whole lot of fun. Home to Shamu, the park's signature killer whale, the facility is the world's largest marine mammal habitat. Lost Lagoon, along with such fun-filled water rides as the Rio Loco and Texas Splashdown, combines with dolphin, sea lion, walrus, harbor seal, and killer whale shows to offer endless family entertainment.

Polar bears and penguins in Texas? Where else but at the San Antonio Zoological Gardens and Aquarium, a mainstay of Brackenridge Park. With more than 3,000 animals representing more than 700 species, the zoo, which opened in 1914, is noted for its captive breeding program and its conservation efforts.

SAN ANTONIO

Texas ranching once was reserved for the trademark longhorn, rounded up by generations of cowboys on horseback. Today's ranchers are more likely to survey their land in four-wheel-drive vehicles, and the state's ubiquitous cattle have had to make room for their more exotic long-necked counterparts.

A Cultural Tapestry

106

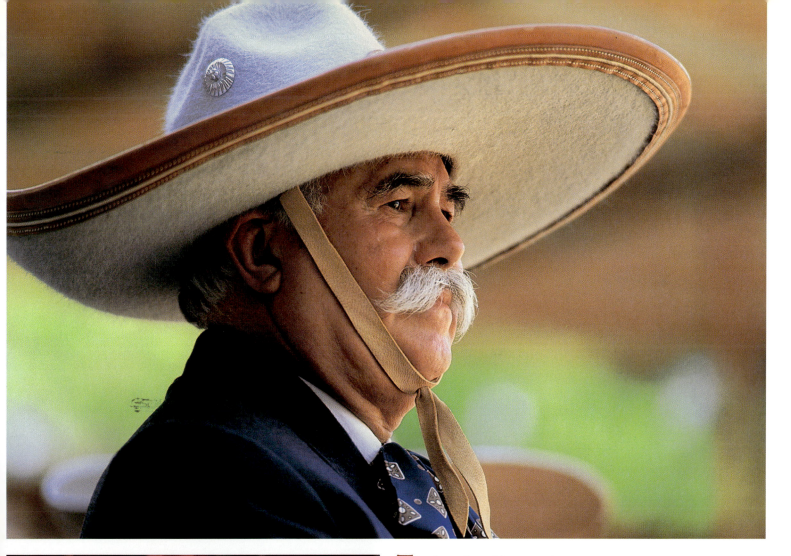

The *charreada*, or Mexican rodeo, is a favorite Sunday afternoon custom in San Antonio. Carrying on the tradition of their ancestors, colorful *charros* put their unique stamp on the ropin' and ridin' skills later made famous by the cowboys in the Old West.

Rodeos offer San Antonians the thrills and spills of bull riding, barrel racing, and a wide range of bronco-busting entertainment. From the arenas that dot the area, riders buck up in anticipation of the San Antonio Stock Show & Rodeo, held annually in the Freeman Coliseum.

Although agriculture today is big business indeed—made up of high-tech corporations, state-of-the-art research, and sophisticated farming techniques—plenty of locals do their part to keep the romance of the past alive. Exhausted from *his* taste of the old days, a bull rider settles down for a little shut-eye (OPPOSITE).

In the early days of cattle trading, deals were sealed by a gentleman's agreement, and financed by gold and silver. Today's livestock go to the highest bidder at auction in the modern version of one of San Antonio's oldest businesses, the Union Stock Yards.

Where's the beef? Much of it makes its way to vendor booths at one of the many events that fill San Antonio's calendar and make the city unique.

A CULTURAL TAPESTRY

115

T he annual Texas Folklife Festival, also known as the World's Biggest Block Party, is the granddaddy of them all. Held each August on the grounds of the Institute of Texan Cultures, the festivities include ethnic foods, exhibits, and craft demonstrations.

With an emphasis on educating the community, the Folklife Festival began in 1972. From down-home fiddlers to Lebanese belly dancers, entertainment representing the 27 nationalities that settled the state of Texas emanates from the event's stages.

M ariachis and colorful Mexican dancers are always in demand at parties and festivals throughout the city, where everyone is encouraged to join in the fun. San Antonians are justly proud of their city's reputation as the epitome of "Tejas," the Native American word for "friend" and the origin of the state's name.

The vibrant sounds of accordian-based *conjunto* music have been a vital part of San Antonio's Tex-Mex culture for many years. One of the sound's early pioneers was Hall of Famer Fred Zimmerle, a prolific recording artist from the late 1940s until his death in 1998 (OPPOSITE). Playing a traditional version of the distinctive style, Santiago Jimenez Jr. (ABOVE) has followed in the footsteps of his father, Santiago Sr., who is widely regarded as the founder of *conjunto*.

A part of the local landscape since 1929, the richly appointed Majestic Theatre on Houston Street is home to the San Antonio Symphony. Through the efforts of Las Casas Foundation, the 1989 restoration of the building's original Moorish design has resulted in a breathtaking visual experience. The Majestic's rich, jewel-toned colors and outstanding acoustics make it one of the finest concert halls in the United States.

A Cultural Tapestry 123

SAN ANTONIO

From fiddlin' with a local flair to opera with an international aura, the city's many stages reflect the diversity of its arts community. Long known as San Antonio's First Lady of Song, Rosita Fernandez (OPPOSITE BOTTOM) has charmed generations of local listeners—not to mention movie stars and presidents—with her hypnotic ballads in English and Spanish. The Guadalupe Cultural Arts Center (BOTTOM), yet another Fiesta City treasure, provides a performance venue for Hispanic artists, musicians, actors, and writers.

As night descends on San Antonio, the lights of downtown beckon locals and visitors alike to sample all the city has to offer.

Unlike many cities where residents escape to the suburbs after dark, in San Antonio, crowds are drawn to the seductive lights of the River Walk, with its diversity of cafés, watering holes, and other nightspots (THIS PAGE). But for a light show in true Texas style, don't miss the giant boots at North Star Mall, where passersby on Loop 410 learn that the stars in this state aren't always lone (OPPOSITE).

Enchanting any time of year, San Antonio at Christmas illustrates why it is considered one of the most romantic cities in the world. From fireworks over Alamo Plaza (PAGE 130) to holiday cheer at the River Walk (PAGE 131), the city's lights delicately illuminate downtown in a seasonal glow.

Another annual River Walk event is Las Posadas, the commemoration of the journey of Mary and Joseph from Nazareth to Bethlehem. The candlelit procession, led by children costumed as members of the holy family, begins at La Mansión del Río and ends at the Arneson River Theatre, concluding yet another San Antonio tradition until the next year.

SAN ANTONIO

The sights, sounds, and flavors of Germany, Old Mexico, the Wild West, the Deep South—all of these traditions represent the cultural tapestry that is San Antonio, a city of historic stature whose future promises to be as rich as its past.

PROFILES IN EXCELLENCE

A look at the corporations, businesses, professional groups, and community service organizations that have made this book possible. Their stories—offering an informal chronicle of the local business community—are arranged according to the date they were established in San Antonio.

Alamo Community College District ■ Bank One San Antonio
Baptist Health System ■ Bay Networks
Bradfield Properties Realtors ■ Catholic Life Insurance
City Public Service ■ Coldwell Banker D'Ann Harper, REALTORS
Crowne Plaza St. Anthony Hotel ■ Datapoint Corporation
The Dee Howard Co. ■ The Domestic Agency
Euro-Alamo Management, Inc. ■ Frontier Enterprises
GPM Life Insurance Company ■ The Greater San Antonio Chamber of Commerce
HEALTHSOUTH Rehabilitation Institute of San Antonio (RIOSA)
Kinetic Concepts, Inc. ■ Marshall Clegg Associates, Inc. ■ McCombs Enterprises
MMI, Inc. ■ Pape-Dawson Engineers, Inc.
PG&E Gas Transmission, Texas Corporation ■ Phyllis Browning Company
St. Mary's University ■ San Antonio Express-News
San Antonio Federal Credit Union ■ SBC Communications Inc.
Sony Semiconductor Company of America ■ Southwest Business Corporation
Southwest Neon Signs, Inc. ■ Ultramar Diamond Shamrock Corporation
United Services Automobile Association
University of Texas Health Science Center at San Antonio
Valero Energy Corporation ■ Vencor Hospital-San Antonio
Warm Springs Rehabilitation System
Waterman Broadcasting Corporation of Texas

1852 – 1959

1852 St. Mary's University

1865 San Antonio Express-News

1891 Bank One San Antonio

1894 The Greater San Antonio Chamber of Commerce

1896 Marshall Clegg Associates, Inc.

1898 Alamo Community College District

1901 Catholic Life Insurance

1902 Baptist Health System

1909 Crowne Plaza St. Anthony Hotel

1922 United Services Automobile Association

1934 GPM Life Insurance Company

1935 San Antonio Federal Credit Union

1942 City Public Service

1946 Southwest Neon Signs, Inc.

1947 The Dee Howard Co.

1947 Frontier Enterprises

1958 McCombs Enterprises

1959 University of Texas Health Science Center at San Antonio

St. Mary's University

St. Mary's University has its origins in St. Mary's Institute, a tiny preparatory school that was founded in 1852 when four brothers of the Society of Mary stepped off the Indianola stagecoach and opened classes in a room above a livery stable in Military Plaza. Today, St. Mary's is the oldest university in San Antonio, and the oldest and largest Catholic university in Texas and the Southwest. Situated on a 135-acre campus just west of downtown San Antonio, the university consists of five schools: Humanities and Social Sciences; Science, Engineering, and Technology; Business and Administration; Graduate School; and School of Law.

With the addition of a Ph.D. program in counseling in 1989, St. Mary's became the city's first four-year university to bring doctoral-level education to San Antonio. St. Mary's School of Law is the only accredited law school in the San Antonio area, and St. Mary's is the only Catholic University in the Southwest with an AACSB-accredited business school.

Holistic Education

At St. Mary's University, education is a holistic endeavor. Its roots are deeply seated in Marianist and Catholic tradition, but the university serves a diverse student body. Learning takes place formally in the classroom, but also informally through a student's extracurricular activities. Volunteer and community service are a vital part of the St. Mary's education, with students working with the elderly and needy people of San Antonio; tutoring high-risk students; and participating in alternative spring breaks in Mexico and on an Indian reservation in Oklahoma to work, eat, live, and share experiences.

St. Mary's currently has an enrollment of about 4,200 students, and maintains a student/teacher ratio of 17 to 1. This allows more individual attention to students, and helps to create a family atmosphere to help students grow to their full potential. St. Mary's has 180 full-time faculty members; 91 percent have doctoral or terminal degrees in their fields.

But despite St. Mary's small size, it has not escaped national attention. *U.S. News & World Report*'s America's Best Colleges issue has ranked St. Mary's as one of the best universities in the region. For more than a decade, St. Mary's has also ranked in the top 10 nationally for the number of Mexican-American students accepted into medical schools.

The vision of St. Mary's is twofold: The university is both working to expand the frontiers of knowledge necessary for the challenges of the next century and endeavoring to prepare graduates to make meaningful contributions to society. With this in mind, St. Mary's is committed to providing a Catholic education experience that evokes academic excellence, while integrating liberal studies, professional preparation, and ethical commitment.

Situated on a 135-acre campus just west of downtown San Antonio, St. Mary's is the oldest university in San Antonio, and the oldest and largest Catholic university in Texas and the Southwest.

San Antonio Express-News

WHEN THE *SAN ANTONIO EXPRESS-NEWS* WAS FOUNDED AS the *San Antonio Express* on September 27, 1865, its presses were powered by a waterwheel, and daily circulation was about 500. It was only one of several newspapers serving a community that then numbered about 10,000 people.

The *San Antonio Express-News* of today is a remarkably different operation. The newspaper utilizes the latest in satellite and computer technology, as well as the most modern color presses available, and has a weekday circulation of 237,558, with 374,481 on Sunday. San Antonio itself has grown into a city of 1.4 million people—the second-largest city in Texas.

In 1993, a 112-year-long circulation contest between the city's two competing dailies was ended when the Hearst Corporation bought the *Express-News* from Rupert Murdoch's News Corporation. Hearst then discontinued publication of the *San Antonio Light*. Many of the *Light*'s features and employees became part of the *Express-News*. In 1996, the *Express-News* launched a marketing campaign to outline its transformed products. "Our mission is to continue to be the primary information source for San Antonio and South Texas," says Edward Prisco, senior vice president of sales, marketing, and new media.

Nearly 1,100 people are employed by the *Express-News*, whose campus covers more than two and a half square blocks of downtown San Antonio. The company completed a $90 million printing facility in 1995, and a state-of-the-art newsroom was dedicated in 1996.

The *Express-News* provides comprehensive coverage of news affecting the nation, region, and community. Daily features, covering the spectrum from personal finance and education to food and wine to religion and spirituality, highlight the publication. The communications company also publishes nearly a dozen niche products, including the *San Antonio Suns*, a group of weekly community newspapers, and *Fiesta Magazine*, a monthly guide targeting visitors to the Alamo City. In addition to daily home delivery and newsstand sales, the *Express-News* offers subscribers electronic delivery via an Internet service provider called EN Connect, and an accompanying Web site at www.expressnews.com.

The company maintains its visibility in the community in many other ways, as well. Through the Newspapers in Education program, the *Express-News* is distributed free, or at reduced fees, to students at local schools. The newspaper offers an opportunity to all local not-for-profit organizations to request space in the paper to promote a special function or benefit. Since 1985, the *Express-News* Charitable Foundation has aided hundreds of local not-for-profit organizations. In 1989, the company raised more than $80,000 to build a playground for inner-city children, and recruited more than 8,000 volunteers to build it.

Through its coverage of news and topics of interest in the San Antonio area, as well as its support of community events, the *San Antonio Express-News* lives up to its motto daily as The One You Turn To.

THE *SAN ANTONIO EXPRESS-NEWS* OF TODAY UTILIZES THE LATEST IN SATELLITE AND COMPUTER TECHNOLOGY, AS WELL AS THE MOST MODERN COLOR PRESSES AVAILABLE, AND HAS A WEEKDAY CIRCULATION OF 237,558, WITH 374,481 ON SUNDAY. A RECENTLY RELEASED REPORT FROM THE DISTINGUISHED SYNDICATED SCARBOROUGH REPORTS SHOWS *SAN ANTONIO EXPRESS-NEWS* AS HAVING THE HIGHEST READERSHIP PENETRATION OF ANY NEWSPAPER IN THE TOP 50 MARKETS IN THE UNITED STATES.

Bank One San Antonio

N 1890, A GROUP OF MOSTLY GERMAN AND ALSATIAN MERCHANTS gathered in the Hugo and Schmeltzer Wholesale Grocery Company, which occupied an adobe building that was part of the historic Alamo mission, to organize a new national bank. Founded in 1891 as the Alamo National Bank, the institution first opened on Texas Independence Day, March 2. The bank has always been located on Commerce Street, first in the Kampmann Building and, since 1930, in its own distinctive 1929 Texas Deco facility at St. Mary's and Commerce streets.

Technology, Training, and Service

The bank became Bank One in 1989, and today emphasizes innovation in technology and services, and continuing education and training for its employees. It was the first bank in the nation to have its own credit card and the first to offer automatic teller machines. "We have always been known as a technology leader," says Charles Lutz, president of Bank One. "It is profound in every aspect of the Bank One companies today."

The bank that began in a grocery store was the first to put a national full-service banking facility in San Antonio grocery stores. "We don't wait for people to come to us—we go to them," Lutz says. Express-banking facilities and automated consumer loan machines in convenient locations are other examples of how Bank One offers services where customers need them most.

The bank's philosophy, "banking one to one," utilizes its leading-edge technology to offer individualized solutions for clients' banking needs at every stage in life. "We're going to offer personal service no matter how sophisticated the equipment becomes," says Lutz. "We are continually changing and evolving. Things don't get predictable. We always are looking for better ways to do our job."

Continuing education in the areas of new products, management, service, and sales training keep employees well trained to make good decisions. "Quality is paramount in this company," says Lutz.

Through Bank One San Antonio, customers have access to all the services of BANC ONE CORPORATION, based in Columbus, Ohio, and one of the top 10 banking institutions in the nation. Leasing, mortgage, securities, and investment advising are among the services available. "The company realizes the value of dedicating all of those resources for the San Antonio community," says Lutz. "We've built a team of people here who are committed to the best deployment of those resources."

Bank One is also committed to the San Antonio community at large, deploying One-der Workers to support activities in the areas of education, at-risk youth, economic development, affordable housing, arts, and culture. "Good corporate citizenship is a strong part of who we think we need to be," says Lutz.

Technology, training, and a complete range of customer services ensure that Bank One will continue to be an important part of the San Antonio community, as it has been for more than a century.

WITH A HISTORY IN SAN ANTONIO DATING BACK TO 1891, BANK ONE HAS BEEN LOCATED IN ITS OWN DISTINCTIVE 1929 TEXAS DECO FACILITY AT ST. MARY'S AND COMMERCE STREETS SINCE 1930.

Alamo Community College District

Most residents of San Antonio are within easy driving distance of a college that is part of Alamo Community College District (ACCD). Created in 1945, after the merger of St. Philip's College and San Antonio Junior College, ACCD today is comprised of four colleges: St. Philip's College, San Antonio College, Palo Alto College, and Northwest Vista College.

ACCD, whose enrollment encompasses more than half of all local college students, is among the most affordable institutions of higher learning in Texas. Tuition averages about 75 percent of the cost of attending a four-year state university, and open admission makes a college education accessible to anyone with a high school diploma. ACCD also serves many nontraditional students, and offers developmental education for students not yet qualified for college work.

The Four Colleges

St. Philip's College, founded in 1898, offers courses that include arts and sciences, business technology, health careers, computer maintenance technology, and interior design. Students attending the Southwest Campus near Kelly Air Force Base can choose from aircraft technology, diesel technology, and welding, among others. St. Philip's also offers Federal Aviation Administration certification courses for airframe technology.

San Antonio College (SAC) is the largest educational institution in the city, with an enrollment of nearly 22,000 students in the spring of 1997. Opened in 1925 as a junior college branch of the University of Texas, SAC later became part of the San Antonio public school system, before joining with St. Philip's to form ACCD.

The members of the teaching faculty at SAC have attained master's degrees or higher, and the college offers more than 68 programs of study. SAC has the area's largest vocational nursing program, a women's center developed to help students with child care and other issues, and a continuing education division that enrolls more than 15,000 students each year.

Palo Alto College (PAC), opened in September 1985, is the only higher education facility in south San Antonio. The college's Student Learning Assistance Center provides computer-aided instruction and individualized help, with full-time tutors in math and English. Many of the courses at PAC are eligible for transfer, and the college offers an associate of applied science degree in majors including horticulture, aviation technology, and biotechnology.

The newest college of ACCD, Northwest Vista College, emphasizes technology, international perspectives, allied health, workforce development programs, and partnerships with educational and business entities. Opened in fall 1995, Northwest Vista teams with local businesses, including Sony Semiconductor of America and VLSI Technology, to train students to meet the needs of the local high-tech industry.

Since Dr. Robert W. Ramsay became chancellor of ACCD in 1993, enrollment has increased from 31,000 to 38,000. Displaced Kelly Air Force Base personnel are creating a demand in the San Antonio area for retraining and higher education; as the city continues to attract high-tech companies, an even greater need for educational services will emerge. The colleges of the Alamo Community College District are poised to meet that demand, and are committed to providing the San Antonio community with affordable and accessible educational opportunities.

The colleges of the Alamo Community College District are committed to providing the San Antonio community with affordable and accessible educational opportunities.

The Greater San Antonio Chamber of Commerce

For more than 100 years, The Greater San Antonio Chamber of Commerce has worked to improve the quality of life and the well-being of San Antonio and the surrounding area through strategic alliances and partnerships. Since its founding in 1894, The Chamber has had a hand in the creation and growth of nearly every major commercial and governmental enterprise in San Antonio. The influence of today's chamber on the city's infrastructure and economy has moved San Antonio toward achieving a potential that the original chamber founders might never have thought possible.

An Indelible Imprint on the Economy

San Antonio's top economic generator continues to be the military. Chamber officials first laid the groundwork for the city's five military bases in 1917, when The Chamber held nearly 8,000 acres of land under option for Kelly Air Force Base. That same year, it assembled another parcel of land, which later became Brooks Air Force Base. During the 1920s, The Chamber also developed a plan to purchase land for Randolph Air Force Base. Eventually, Kelly AFB became San Antonio's largest employer. One of the oldest continuously active military installations in the country, it employs nearly 5,200 military personnel and more than 13,000 civilians.

When the Base Realignment and Closure program (BRAC) threatened San Antonio's military installations nearly 70 years later, The Chamber created a community-wide coalition to save Kelly Air Force Base. As a major project during The Chamber's 1994 centennial, the organization's Forward San Antonio initiative raised $2.7 million to fund margin of excellence programs such as the BRAC 1995 effort to facilitate the reuse and privatization of Kelly facilities once its closure was finalized. The Chamber supported the efforts of the Greater Kelly Development Corporation to successfully persuade the Boeing Company to establish a major aerospace logistics and support center for large aircraft at Kelly Air Force Base.

Making Tourism Tops

The Chamber's efforts have helped make tourism the city's second-largest economic generator. In 1911, the organization created the Fiesta Association. Later renamed the

Clockwise from left:

While San Antonio's history dates to the late 1600s, much of its commercial infrastructure is modern, such as this office building on the north side, at the intersection of two major highways, IH-10 and IH-410.

Chamber president and CEO Joe Krier

The new downtown campus of the University of Texas San Antonio, begun in 1996, promises to be the catalyst for the revitalization of the near west side of San Antonio.

Fiesta San Antonio Commission, it oversees the annual 10-day spring extravaganza known as Fiesta. During the 1950s, a chamber committee studied the feasibility of pursuing an international World's Fair, which eventually brought HemisFair '68 to San Antonio. Another chamber group began studies for a river development program, which led to the Paseo del Rio project. An improved San Antonio River Walk, one of the city's best-loved tourist attractions, was the result.

In addition, chamber officials were involved in creating the Alamodome, a multipurpose facility that seats up to 65,000 and can be configured for sporting events, trade shows, and other large-scale events. Other entities The Chamber has been instrumental in founding include the San Antonio Sports Foundation, created to attract professional and amateur sporting events to San Antonio, and the San Antonio Livestock Exposition.

Less visible, but just as vital, have been The Chamber's efforts on behalf of the community's infrastructure. For more than 50 years, chamber highway and transportation committees have developed plans to create or augment local highway systems. Chamber leadership and support of the McAllister Freeway, improvements to Interstates 35 and 10 downtown, Highway 151, and other major roadway projects have helped the city's streets and highways keep pace with its growth. "Today, The Chamber is forcefully advocating long-term highway and transportation improvements that will benefit us well into the next century," says 1998 Chamber Chairman Nelson Wolff.

EDUCATION, INTERNATIONAL BUSINESS ARE KEY

Education has been a major focus of The Chamber for many years.

In 1942, chamber officials worked to relocate Trinity University to San Antonio from Waxahachie. Thirty chamber members appeared before a state coordinating board in 1968 to lobby for a state-supported university, a college of dentistry, and a nursing school in San Antonio. This effort was instrumental in the establishment of the South Texas Medical Center. Today, the center is a $1.3 billion, 800-acre complex that includes the University of Texas Health Science Center at San Antonio, major health care institutions, freestanding research centers, and numerous facilities that provide health education, treatment, and research. The medical industry is the third-largest economic generator in San Antonio. In addition, The Chamber has supported bond issues at the college level, and creation of the San Antonio Education Partnership to promote excellence in academics and attendance at public schools. "Our future economy is dependent on strong systems of public and higher education," says 1999 Board Chairman-Elect Arthur Emerson.

The Chamber also works with the city's leading enterprises to facilitate commerce with Mexico and other nations. Through trips

to Mexico, Laredo, and Washington, D.C., in 1991, The Chamber helped ensure fast-track authority for a proposed free-trade agreement with Mexico. In 1992, the North American Free Trade Agreement (NAFTA) was signed in San Antonio. "We have a great opportunity to become a center of international trade, to be an inland port," comments Chamber President and CEO Joe Krier.

Today, The Greater San Antonio Chamber of Commerce continues to act as a catalyst for economic development in San Antonio, playing a key role in establishing businesses, organizations, and capital projects that make the city an economic powerhouse and the number one tourist destination in Texas. For more than 100 years, The Chamber has been working as a strong, effective voice for business.

SENT BY THE KING OF SPAIN IN 1731 ON THE PREMISE THAT 15 FAMILIES COULD DO MORE GOOD THAN 100 SOLDIERS, CANARY ISLANDERS ESTABLISHED VILLA DE FERNANDO AS THE FIRST CIVILIAN MUNICIPALITY IN TEXAS; SAN FERNANDO CATHEDRAL IN MAIN PLAZA SOON FOLLOWED, AND IS STILL STANDING (LEFT).

THE SAN ANTONIO RIVER WALK, A WELCOME RESPITE FROM THE HUSTLE OF MODERN CITY LIFE, IS THE NUMBER ONE TOURIST DESTINATION IN TEXAS, AND THE CENTER OF COMMERCE FOR MANY LOCAL AND NATIONAL HOTEL AND RESTAURANT CHAINS (RIGHT).

MARSHALL CLEGG ASSOCIATES, INC.

ALMOST ANYPLACE YOU LOOK, MARSHALL CLEGG ASSOCIATES, Inc.'s downtown office-furniture facility is surrounded by history. Each year, the family business, which started in 1896, makes some history of its own. Step down into a computer design area that once was a printing plant, and you walk past a rusting cannonball laying on the floor. Marshall Clegg says it was unearthed early in the century, when the city razed the Veramendi home that stood on the Soledad Street frontage owned by his grandfather, L.B. Clegg. Clegg adds that the artifact had been around for some time before he learned General Antonio López de Santa Anna had aimed a cannon at the Alamo from the site during the famous 1836 siege.

The business doesn't go back quite that far, but it does go back to when Luther Bynum Clegg bought a one-third interest in San Antonio Printing Co., which had opened in 1896. L.B. Clegg gained control of the firm in 1906, and at about the same time expanded into the office furniture and supply business. The firm, renamed The Clegg Co. in the 1920s, continued until Marshall Clegg bought the furniture business in the early 1970s, while a brother took the printing operation.

CHANGING WITH THE TIMES

Today, more than 102 years after the original company's founding, Marshall Clegg Associates, Inc. ranks as one of San Antonio's largest commercial furniture firms, with annual sales rates in the $25 million range.

As times have changed, Clegg says, so have offices—and so has his product line. "I don't think anybody understood what the effect of the computer would be," he says, adding that today, even executives need a computer on their desks. Change not only has been extensive, but it is accelerating. "For years and years, you had a slow rate of change," adds Clegg.

But traditional furniture is still available for those who want it. "There are companies that make rolltop desks. The problem is, the needs of the office don't relate back to being solved by that type of equipment," says Clegg.

In the old days, an architect might design an office, and its occupant would shop for furniture to fill it, often with little regard to relating furniture with function. That began to change with Robert Propst's 1968 book titled *The Office: A Facility Based on Change*. The Herman Miller Co. designed a line of contemporary office furniture based on the book's ideas, and Clegg began selling it as a Herman

CLOCKWISE FROM TOP:
MARSHALL CLEGG ASSOCIATES, INC. GOES BACK TO WHEN LUTHER BYNUM CLEGG BOUGHT A ONE-THIRD INTEREST IN SAN ANTONIO PRINTING CO., WHICH HAD OPENED IN 1896. SEVERAL YEARS LATER, HE EXPANDED INTO THE OFFICE FURNITURE AND SUPPLY BUSINESS.

THIRD-GENERATION OWNER AND PRESIDENT MARSHALL T. CLEGG STANDS WITH HIS GRANDSON, THE COMPANY'S POSSIBLE FUTURE OWNER AND PRESIDENT, DANIEL CLEGG MITCHELL.

THE CURRENT CLEGG FACILITY IS LOCATED ON THE SITE OF THE OLD VERAMENDI PALACE (ON LEFT); CLEGG'S ORIGINAL HEADQUARTERS, WHICH THE COMPANY OCCUPIED FROM 1896 UNTIL 1910, IS SHOWN TO THE RIGHT IN THE PHOTOGRAPH.

THE CLEGG CO. FURNISHED CLASSIC OFFICES IN THE MID-1920S.

Miller dealer. "It's a whole new process of thinking how people can relate together," Clegg explains.

Modular office furniture incorporating work surfaces, dividers, and file cabinets can be broken down, then reconfigured and reinstalled to help a business make new use of old space and fixtures.

Clegg began using modular "systems furniture" concepts in 1968. Since then, systems furniture has undergone an evolution. Today, electrical wiring, specialized wiring for data, and fiber optics for computer networking must be accommodated in the furniture system.

"The biggest changes I have seen have been the result of the computer introduction," says Clegg. "Computers and peripherals have changed the needs of the working environment completely, as well as the ability to plan these new environments. Adds Clegg, "Before systems furniture, it was difficult to accommodate the changes. With systems furniture, you can build it to do what you need it to do. If that doesn't work, you can efficiently redo it again."

Because of the nature of systems furniture, the installation of the project has become more complex. In effect, each workstation is built on the job site. Clegg provides not only designers but project managers, account coordinators, installation supervisors, and foremen who plan and coordinate every phase of the project, even trading in the old products.

Much of the company's 50,000 square feet of downtown space is devoted to office showrooms. One can find functional work spaces along with sumptuous simulated executive suites. "We use these showrooms to teach people how the products go together," Clegg says.

Besides occupying restored space in the company's 1910 vintage building, the showrooms spill over into lease space at an even older rock structure next door that was once a hotel. Overall, the remodeled downtown buildings—like the furniture inside them—remain functional to this day, with high ceilings and ample lighting.

The main structure also backs up to the River Walk, where a second-story balcony overlooks some stately cypress trees Clegg's grandfather helped transplant decades ago.

The grandson of the man who founded the company more than 100 years ago is proud of the Clegg reputation for good work and responsible business practices, but modestly points out that it was established long before he entered the picture. The future, as Clegg sees it, holds more of the same: "Staying up to date is important. People want to be able to discuss their furniture needs with someone who can help them incorporate into their offices the solutions to current issues affecting the office environment—whether it's wiring for workstations or being information leaders in office ergonomics."

SYSTEMS FURNITURE PROVIDES AN EFFECTIVE WORK ENVIRONMENT WHILE MANAGING ALL OF THE CABLES AND WIRES OF ADVANCED TECHNOLOGY. THE CABLES, NEATLY TUCKED INTO PANELS OF THE SYSTEMS FURNITURE, REMAIN HIDDEN FROM VIEW.

Catholic Life Insurance

Nearly a century ago, a group of German immigrants who wanted to help their neighbors in time of need founded a small benevolent society. Created to provide life insurance for those unable to secure coverage from already existing companies, this society met a growing need for Texas settlers at the turn of the century.

Today, Catholic Life Insurance is an organization with more than 70,000 certificate holders, more than $350 million in assets, $1.6 billion in insurance, and an Excellent rating from analyst A.M. Best Co.

Serving a Special Niche

Life was hard and money was scarce for German Catholics in Texas around the turn of the century. When someone died, neighbors passed the hat to raise what little money they could for the survivors. But even with a helping hand, loss of the breadwinner often spelled financial ruin for a family.

Life insurance was too costly for most settlers, and it was difficult for farmers, with their uncertain incomes, to get coverage from insurance companies. Certain fraternal benefit societies offered affordable life insurance, but too often their rituals conflicted with Catholic belief.

In 1901, under the leadership of Monsignor Henry Gerlach, the German Catholics formed their own fraternal benefit group, Deutsch Romisch Katholischen Staatsverband für Texas, later called the Catholic State League. The incorporators of this organization included some of the families who helped build Texas: Anton Kalich of High Hill; William Kleypas and John C. Bockholt of Westphalia; Charles Skarke of Galveston; and J.C. Dielmann, George Mandry, B.J. Lang, and Frank Lang of San Antonio.

The Staatsverband, based on a legal reserve system, drafted a constitution and bylaws. On November 25, 1901, a requisite 100 applicants had signed up for coverage, and a charter was granted by the State of Texas to the Sterbekasse der Deutschen Katholiken von Texas—the Death Fund of the German Catholics of Texas. The charter of the San Antonio-based organization stated that its purpose was "to organize and incorporate a fraternal benefit association for the sole benefit of its members and beneficiaries, and not for profit."

On January 1, 1902, the first life insurance certificate was issued to Gerlach; by the end of the day, 62 other certificates had been issued. At first, protection was restricted to Staatsverband members and their families. Members paid no dues and no membership fees, a policy the company maintains today.

Steady Growth

Caution and conservatism limited growth in the early years, but by 1915, membership was at 305, with $159,000 worth of insurance in force. Twenty years later, membership had swelled to 1,071, with $892,000 of coverage in force.

Each year, Catholic Life Insurance celebrates Flag Day, the birth of our nation's flag, by raising a 110- by 55-foot United States flag at its corporate headquarters (left).

Catholic Life Insurance traces its origins to the Catholic State League of Texas, a religious and civic organization for German Catholics. In 1898, the founders of the Catholic State League gathered in nearby Castroville (right).

In 1936, the company name was changed to Catholic Life Insurance Union.

When Catholic Life Insurance celebrated its 50th birthday in 1951, the organization had more than 15,000 members, $12 million worth of insurance in force, and assets totaling more than $1.7 million. Additional financial services were added, the limits of coverage were broadened, and membership was opened to any Catholic residing in Texas.

July 1975 marked two milestones for Catholic Life Insurance. The amount of insurance topped $100 million, and the company, which had outgrown several previous homes, relocated to a nine-story building on Loop 410.

The 1980s was a time of major growth and change for the company. Assets and insurance-in-force continued to increase, while products and services were made available to non-Catholics.

A Legacy of Firsts

Over the years, Catholic Life Insurance has been an innovator in the insurance industry. From its inception, the company made life insurance available to women, becoming one of the first groups to do so. In 1909, when it began offering home loans, Catholic Life Insurance was one of Bexar County's first mortgage lenders. In 1994, the company became the first mortgage lender in Texas to pay interest on escrow accounts.

Today, solid individual and group life insurance plans, as well as IRAs and retirement annuities, comprise Catholic Life Insurance's core products. These products are complemented by strong fraternal and "living" benefits.

"What really separates us from other life insurers is our living benefits program," says J. Michael Belz, president and CEO. "Most are provided at no additional cost." They include an additional $2,500 to survivors of any member who dies accidentally, and payment of up to $25,000 additionally if a member owning an annuity dies accidentally. Members may also use a percentage of their annuity cash value to pay for nursing home care, without having to pay surrender penalties.

Other living benefits include assistance for members who are victims of natural disasters or serious illness. Terminally ill members are allowed access to a certain portion of their life insurance benefits. Additionally, Catholic Life Insurance pays up to $200 a month in financial assistance to orphaned children of members; these benefits continue until the child reaches 18 years of age.

Helping Neighbors

Among its many fraternal programs, Catholic Life Insurance provides life insurance for Catholic bishops, with the premiums being paid for by members. When a bishop dies, his life insurance proceeds are used to pay for vocational education for future priests. The company has paid out $100,000 to 40 seminarians, many of whom are now priests. Catholic Life Insurance also awards scholarships to certificate holders to attend Catholic high schools and public or private universities, and provides valuable financial assistance to needy Catholic elementary schools.

Catholic Life Insurance continues its dedication to its core principle of neighbors helping neighbors by offering volunteer opportunities to members in each of the company's branches, which are spread throughout Texas, Louisiana, Oklahoma, and New Mexico.

Today, as its founding members originally intended, Catholic Life Insurance is committed to being a good neighbor while helping families secure their future.

ALTHOUGH MEMBERSHIP IS NO LONGER LIMITED TO CATHOLICS, CATHOLIC LIFE INSURANCE RETAINS ITS SUPPORT OF CATHOLIC TRADITIONS AND ORGANIZATIONS. REVEREND MONSIGNOR LAWRENCE J. STUEBBEN, VICAR GENERAL FOR THE ARCHDIOCESE OF SAN ANTONIO, OFFERS THE ANNUAL MASS FOR LIVING AND DECEASED MEMBERS OF CATHOLIC LIFE INSURANCE (LEFT).

PRESIDENT J. MICHAEL BELZ GREETS ARCHBISHOP PATRICK FLORES, THE LEADER OF THE CATHOLIC CHURCH IN SAN ANTONIO AND SURROUNDING AREAS. CATHOLIC LIFE INSURANCE WORKS CLOSELY WITH CHURCH OFFICIALS THROUGHOUT TEXAS, LOUISIANA, OKLAHOMA, AND NEW MEXICO (RIGHT).

Baptist Health System

The Baptist Health System strives to improve health throughout every phase of a person's life and changing health needs. A recognized health care leader in San Antonio and South Texas, Baptist Health System is a state-of-the-art health care system with two major distinctions: It is a not-for-profit organization and it is dedicated to a mission that includes Christian service. Its five acute care hospitals and other health-related services have a total of 1,566 licensed beds and 2,000 physicians.

As a not-for-profit, community-based organization, Baptist Health System returns all of its revenue over expenses to the local community through improved equipment and services, charity and unreimbursed care, and free community wellness and outreach programs. Through free cancer and heart screenings, and other community health services and unreimbursed patient care, Baptist Health System donates nearly $41 million in charity and unreimbursed services to the city's residents each year. Baptist Health System is the city's only hospital system to be selected for membership in Voluntary Hospitals of America, a nationwide network of leading community-owned health care organizations and physicians.

Locations throughout the City

One of Baptist Health System's greatest strengths is that it is widely accessible to the community through multiple locations. There is a Baptist hospital to serve every sector of San Antonio, including the Baptist Medical Center downtown, North Central Baptist Hospital, Northeast Baptist Hospital, Southeast Baptist Hospital, and St. Luke's Baptist Hospital in the Medical Center.

Beyond the hospital walls, an alternate services division offers preventive medicine, wellness efforts, occupational medicine, and home health care. The expansion of alternate services demonstrates the Baptist Health System's commitment to caring for people during every age and health need. Community health and wellness programs are an important component of the strategic plan. Baptist Health System is committed to making a difference in the community by improving the health status of its residents. The system has dedicated a variety of resources—time, money, and people—toward this goal.

HealthLink-McCreless, a health education resource center at McCreless Mall on the south side of town, presents a variety of free and low-cost health activities each month. The first of five planned wellness and fitness centers—HealthLink-North—was dedicated in 1998. HealthLink is an important part of the Baptist continuum of care—offering fitness facilities to prevent illness and encourage wellness, and rehabilitation facilities to help restore health.

Outreach partnerships like Z-Gym, a collaborative effort between HealthLink and Z-Place, a church-affiliated family center, meet a variety of needs in an impoverished neighborhood in San Antonio. The community looks to the Baptist Health System to be the resource for the prevention of illness and the promotion of wellness.

"Health is much more than the absence of disease," says Fred R. Mills, president and CEO of the Baptist Health System. "Not being sick is not good enough anymore. People want to function at maximum capacity, to enjoy the best life has to offer."

Baptist's Institute of Health Education operates professional and vocational nursing schools and allied health schools, as well as programs for staff development and community health education. Regional health services and ambulatory care centers also are being developed.

"These expanded services will help us care for the health of our patients in the future," says Mills. "We aren't limited by hospital walls any more. We are limited only by the boundaries of our patients' health needs."

Baptist Health System is a state-of-the-art health care system with two major distinctions: It is a not-for-profit organization and it is dedicated to a mission that includes Christian service.

There is a Baptist hospital to serve every sector of San Antonio, including the Baptist Medical Center downtown, North Central Baptist Hospital, Northeast Baptist Hospital, Southeast Baptist Hospital, and St. Luke's Baptist Hospital in the Medical Center.

When Mills joined Baptist Health System in 1996, he developed a five-year plan for the system with input from physicians, administrators, and employees. His Vision 2001 program focuses on developing an integrated delivery system of health that incorporates all aspects of health and wellness. Explains Mills, "It means that anyone with a health need can get the care they need by entering one system."

A History of Commitment to Excellence

This ongoing commitment to excellence in health care started in 1902, when a group of more than 60 physicians and businessmen organized San Antonio Associated Charities, which initiated construction of a four-story hospital downtown. They called it Physicians' and Surgeons' Hospital—popularly known as P&S Hospital.

In 1926, another group of doctors built Medical & Surgical Hospital across the street from Physicians' and Surgeons' Hospital. Following the Great Depression, the competing hospitals found it increasingly difficult to continue offering care with limited funds. They merged in 1944 to form Medical and Surgical Memorial Hospital. The governing board decided a church-affiliated institution could help it better serve the needs of the community. In 1948, the Southern Baptist Convention assumed control and changed the name to Baptist Memorial Hospital.

Continuous upgrading added a series of buildings in the area surrounding the original P&S building. By the time the Baptist General Convention of Texas had assumed ownership in 1952, the Baptist hospital complex had expanded into a modern, fully equipped, total health care center.

Satellite Pioneer

Expansion continued, and Baptist Memorial grew to encompass 7.5

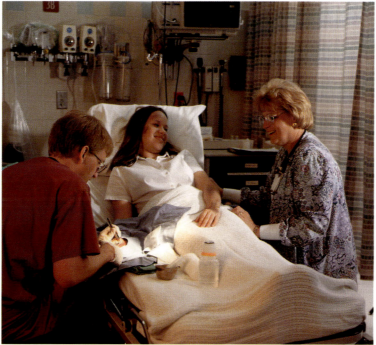

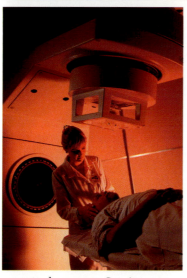

acres in downtown San Antonio. The Baptist Memorial Hospital System was formed with the ground breaking for a second hospital on November 1, 1969, a pioneering step in the concept of satellite hospitals in San Antonio. That satellite, Northeast Baptist Hospital, opened in 1970. A growing commitment to placing health care facilities where people live and work led the system to establish Southeast Baptist Hospital a year later. Over the years, these hospitals ceased to be satellites and grew into full-service facilities.

In 1991, the system opened North Central Baptist Hospital in the planned community of Stone Oak, one of the fastest-growing areas of San Antonio. In 1994, the 17-year-old St. Luke's Lutheran Hospital in the Medical Center area merged with Baptist Health System to become St. Luke's Baptist Hospital.

The hospitals continue to expand to meet the specific needs of their communities while offering comprehensive care. Baptist Medical Center, the first hospital in the city to provide dedicated facilities for the treatment of heart disease, offers complete medical facilities, including cardiac and cancer services, a 24-hour emergency department, dialysis, diabetes care, a skilled nursing facility, and more. A Level III nursery, or intensive care unit for newborns, opened in 1998.

Northeast Baptist Hospital, in early 1997, became the only hospital on the city's northeast side to offer a Level III nursery. The Neonatal Intensive Care Unit at Northeast Baptist Hospital is the only Level III nursery between that side of San Antonio and Austin. Northeast Baptist Hospital offers full cardiac services, 24-hour emergency care, maternity care, pediatric care, and the largest ambulatory

EMERGENCY DEPARTMENTS AT ALL FIVE BAPTIST HEALTH SYSTEM HOSPITALS OFFER 24-HOUR EMERGENCY CARE. CONVENIENTLY LOCATED IN AREAS THROUGHOUT SAN ANTONIO, THESE EMERGENCY DEPARTMENTS OFFER THE ASSURANCE OF ACCESSIBLE EMERGENCY CARE WHEREVER PEOPLE LIVE. A NEW CHILDREN'S EMERGENCY CENTER IN THE NORTH CENTRAL AREA BRINGS SPECIALIZED EMERGENCY CARE TO CHILDREN IN A LOCATION NOT PREVIOUSLY AVAILABLE TO THEM.

CANCER SERVICES ARE OFFERED THROUGHOUT THE BAPTIST HEALTH SYSTEM. THE HEART OF ACUTE CANCER TREATMENT IN THE SYSTEM IS THE BAPTIST CANCER CENTER, THE ONLY HOSPITAL-BASED FACILITY IN SOUTH TEXAS THAT OFFERS RADIATION THERAPY, HIGH-DOSE BRACHYTHERAPY, AND HYPERTHERMIA TREATMENT IN ONE CONVENIENT LOCATION.

SAN ANTONIO AIRLIFE PROVIDES INTENSIVE CARE IN FLIGHT FOR SOUTH TEXAS, AND IS OPERATED BY BAPTIST HEALTH SYSTEM IN PARTNERSHIP WITH THE UNIVERSITY HEALTH SYSTEM (TOP).

WELLNESS, REHABILITATION, AND FITNESS EFFORTS HELP COMPLETE THE CONTINUUM OF CARE OFFERED IN THE BAPTIST HEALTH SYSTEM. OCCUPATIONAL MEDICINE INCLUDES A PHYSICAL REHABILITATION COMPONENT, PICTURED HERE AT THE HEALTHMASTER SERVICES CLINIC. A STATE-OF-THE-ART WELLNESS AND FITNESS CENTER, HEALTHLINK-NORTH BRINGS A NEW DIMENSION IN WELLNESS TO THE PEOPLE OF SAN ANTONIO (BOTTOM).

care center of its kind in San Antonio.

The Baptist Regional Children's Center is located on the campus of North Central Baptist Hospital. It offers care for children from birth to adolescence in an area that accounts for 32 percent of pediatric admissions in the city. A group of the city's leading pediatric subspecialists are located as a multidisciplinary practice in the Remington Oaks Medical Office Building adjacent to the children's center.

North Central Baptist Hospital also offers a wide range of diagnostic, treatment, maternity, and rehabilitation services. Its adult and pediatric emergency departments serve the emergency needs of residents in north central San Antonio and in the region north of the city.

Southeast Baptist Hospital has become an international center for small-incision surgery, frequently hosting physicians from across the nation and around the world for training. It was the first site in San Antonio to offer percutaneous laparoscopic laser cholecystectomy, a technique for gall bladder removal. Southeast Baptist's services include 24-hour emergency care, sports medicine support, a comprehensive range of outpatient and inpatient diagnostic and treatment services, maternity care, intensive care, and a skilled nursing facility.

St. Luke's Baptist Hospital is taking a life-stage approach to its new women's center, to be opened in 1999. This women's center, with complete obstetric and gynecologic services on the campus of St. Luke's, will fill the needs of a dynamic and important segment of the population. The dedicated women's center will be capable of handling more than 2,000 deliveries each year, and will offer a neonatal intensive care unit in addition to care for well babies. St. Luke's offers complete cardiac care services. The Phase I Drug Development Program at St. Luke's is made possible through a National Cancer Institute grant awarded by the Cancer Therapy and Research Center and the University of Texas Health Science Center. Physicians practicing at St. Luke's have pioneered new techniques in cardiology, colorectal surgery, orthopedics, neuroradiology, gynecology, and plastic and microsurgery. St. Luke's also provides 24-hour emergency services, a skilled nursing facility, and a geriatric-psychiatric unit.

COMPREHENSIVE, COHESIVE CARE

Though each Baptist hospital has its specialized programs, many coordinate in specific fields for comprehensive, cohesive care. The Baptist Heart Network has established complete cardiac care services at Baptist Medical Center, Northeast Baptist, and St. Luke's. North Central and Southeast Baptist hospitals are equipped and staffed to diagnose, monitor, and stabilize heart patients until they can be transferred to one of the three Baptist centers of cardiac excellence. The Baptist hospitals are recognized for their expertise in caring for patients with heart problems.

The Baptist Health System offers complete services for cancer patients at all five of its hospitals. The Baptist Cancer Center, adjacent to Baptist Medical Center, is the most comprehensive hospital-based radiation center in South Texas. The Phase I Drug Development Program at St. Luke's is made possible through a National Cancer Institute grant awarded by the Cancer Therapy and Research Center and the University of Texas Health Science Center. In Phase I studies, new anticancer drugs previously tested in the laboratory are given to humans for the first time.

The Baptist system has many additional facilities, services, and affiliates to further its mission of Christian care and service. Its air medical transport service, San Antonio AirLife, provides intensive care in flight for South Texas, operated in partnership with the University Health System. Baptist Health System participates in the Texas Trauma Program, which facilitates bringing rural patients in a 24-county area to San Antonio for treatment.

The San Antonio Eye Bank handles eye donations and provides corneas for transplant in San Antonio and other regional communities. The system is expanding Baptist Home Health Services to make care more accessible and affordable. Baptist Health System also has developed an international relations staff to meet the special needs of patients from Latin America.

Focus on Patient Care

Though the range of services and quality of care are undisputedly among the best in the city, a systemwide commitment to focusing on patient care seems to make the biggest impression on Baptist patrons. System employees—including nurses, technicians, business office workers, and others—are instilled with the understanding that their interaction with the patient has an impact.

"Excellent medical care is basic to our mission, and it is what people expect of us when they come to our doors," says Mills. But, he adds, there is more to caring for patients than the medical care they receive. "Service excellence is an important part of the attention we give," he asserts. "Service excellence has to do with how we treat our patients, visitors, and each other. It can set us apart from other health care providers and make us the system of choice in San Antonio and South Texas.

"We work with every employee to instill a desire to view every patient as a family member and to provide ways to give the best service possible," says Mills. Today, according to consumer surveys, more people in San Antonio say they would choose a Baptist hospital than any other hospital. Baptist's long-standing focus on individual patients, as well as on their families and the community as a whole, continues to make a difference.

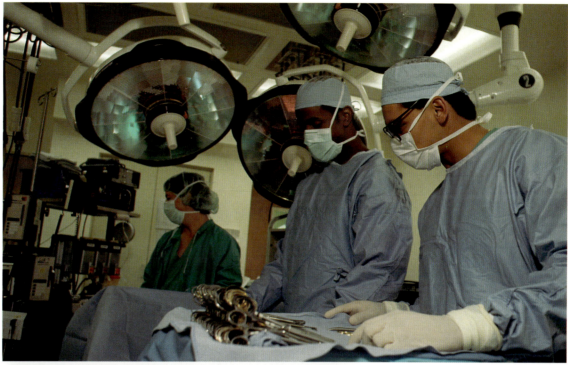

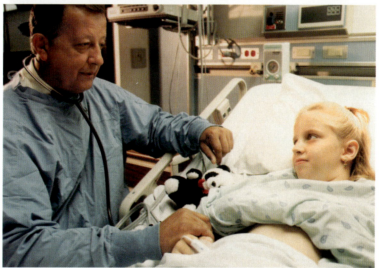

"Excellent medical care is basic to our mission, and it is what people expect of us when they come to our doors," says Fred R. Mills, president and CEO of the Baptist Health System. Open heart surgery, like that shown above, is an example of the sophisticated care given in the Baptist Health System.

On the campus of North Central Baptist Hospital, the Baptist Regional Children's Center provides pediatric services for children from birth through adolescence, with next-door proximity to some of the finest pediatric subspecialists in South Texas (bottom).

CROWNE PLAZA ST. ANTHONY HOTEL

IN 1909, CATTLEMEN F.M. SWEARINGEN, B.L. NAYLOR, AND A.H. Jones (who would later become mayor of San Antonio) built the St. Anthony Hotel to capitalize on the city's rich history, diverse culture, and unique architecture. They began with a $100,000 investment, and selected the name St. Anthony to acknowledge the city's history. The hotel quickly became the province of oil barons, movie stars, and kings.

Today, the hotel is the Crowne Plaza St. Anthony Hotel, and it sits in the heart of downtown San Antonio. Expanded from one original eight-story tower to two towers and then three, the hotel now has 352 guest rooms, each individually decorated with antiques. "Each room has its own charm," says Peter Ells, general manager of the hotel. "We appeal to people who want something different than a typical hotel stay."

HISTORIC IN CHARACTER

A mix of the historical and the modern, the St. Anthony features French decor, with Italian marble wainscoting and entry stairs, and Venetian mosaic tile in the lobby. The hotel boasts a business center, a fitness center, and all of the room amenities of a contemporary facility. "We have all of the modern amenities and conveniences, but we've managed to keep the historic charm of the hotel," says Ells.

The hotel has itself made history through the years. During the Great Depression, the city of San Antonio experienced hard times, and the St. Anthony Hotel went into foreclosure. The man who is credited with saving the hotel and transforming it into the premier hotel of the Southwest, Ralph W. Morrison, bought the St. Anthony in 1936. Under Morrison's direction, extensive renovations made the St. Anthony the first hotel ever to be completely and continuously air-conditioned; the first to have a drive-up, garage-level registration desk; and the first to use electric-eye, automatic opening doors.

Morrison also purchased many of the hotel's French Empire antiques, and commissioned original oil and watercolor paintings from such noted artists as Frederic Remington and Harry Anthony DeYoung. When renovations were finalized around 1941, the hotel became known as the "Waldorf on the prairie."

The St. Anthony saw its heyday in the decades following Morrison's acquisition and renovation. Gentleman guests were required to wear a coat and tie in the grand lobby, which to this day features treasures collected from around the world and eight-foot, Empire-style chandeliers. The garage allowed visitors to drive their cars in, then take the elevator up to their room to change before entering the main lobby,

CLOCKWISE FROM TOP:
THE CROWNE PLAZA ST. ANTHONY HOTEL SITS IN THE HEART OF DOWNTOWN SAN ANTONIO.

THE ST. ANTHONY OFFERS 352 SPACIOUS GUEST ROOMS AND SUITES BEAUTIFULLY APPOINTED WITH ANTIQUE FURNISHINGS AND MODERN AMENITIES.

PRICELESS ANTIQUES, TAPESTRIES, AND OLD PAINTINGS ADORN THE FAMOUS PROMENADE KNOWN AS PEACOCK ALLEY.

CLOCKWISE FROM TOP LEFT:
THE GRAND STYLE AND ARCHITECTURE OF THE ANACACHO BALLROOM MAKE IT ONE OF THE MOST POPULAR BALLROOMS IN SAN ANTONIO.

ONCE AN EXCLUSIVE PRIVATE CLUB, THE ST. ANTHONY CLUB ROOM IS A FAVORITE FOR SOCIAL EVENTS.

THE GEORGIAN ROOM, AN ELEGANT JUNIOR BALLROOM, IS AN EXCELLENT EXAMPLE OF THE UNIQUE AMBIENCE OF THE ST. ANTHONY.

where the parade of well-turned-out women earned it the name Peacock Alley.

San Antonio became a hub of military activity during World War II, and many Hollywood luminaries visited the St. Anthony to support the war effort. Photographs chronicling visits of such notables as Jeanette McDonald, Rosalind Russell, and Fred Astaire adorn the hotel's walls. Eleanor Roosevelt, General Douglas MacArthur, and President Dwight Eisenhower were also among those who visited Peacock Alley during the war years.

A million-dollar renovation in 1959 brought renewed elegance to the hotel, and a lush private club was added at the suggestion of Dorothy Draper, an internationally renowned decorator. The St. Anthony Club became one of the first in the nation to draw members from around the globe, one of whom was President Lyndon Johnson. Called the Nightclub of the Southwest, it featured top bands each week and broadcast live performances to radio fans. The St. Anthony Club hosted celebrities including Princess Grace of Monaco, Gregory Peck, Rock Hudson, and John Wayne, who lived at the hotel for a year during the filming of *The Alamo* in nearby Brackettville.

The Morrison family sold the St. Anthony Hotel in 1971. Ten years later, it was sold to Intercontinental Hotels, and in 1988, it came under the management of Park Lane Hotels International. A 1996, multimillion-dollar renovation refurbished all hotel guest rooms. Sunday brunches are still a grand affair at the hotel and are held in Peacock Alley. The Anacacho Ballroom, with glittering chandeliers, mirrors, and an ornate second-floor balcony, is a center for social events for prominent local families.

EVERY GUEST IS A STAR

In fulfilling its modern mission to provide excellent customer service, strive for continuous improvement, and preserve its history, the Crowne Plaza St. Anthony Hotel continues to welcome today's celebrities. In October 1995, the hotel hosted guests in town for the grand opening of Planet Hollywood on the San Antonio River Walk, including Demi Moore, Bruce Willis, George Clooney, Arnold Schwarzenegger, Charlie Sheen, Luke Perry, and others.

But the hotel remains ever mindful of the loyal guests who have contributed to its near-century of history. With this in mind, the St. Anthony honors couples who have celebrated honeymoons or anniversaries there by inviting them back for a stay at the rate they originally paid. In 1997, an Abilene couple returned to mark their 50th anniversary, and were charged the rate listed on their original hotel bill—$7 per night.

As it was when it opened, the St. Anthony Hotel remains an oasis of charm and beauty for royalty and business travelers alike. With a firm footing in the past and a firm grasp on the future, the St. Anthony Hotel is poised to enter its second century as a leader in deluxe accommodations in San Antonio.

A CULTURAL TAPESTRY

United Services Automobile Association

In 1922, Major William H. Garrison Jr. called a meeting of his fellow army officers at San Antonio's Gunter Hotel. The officers gathered together to discuss their common need for economical and reliable automobile insurance. Because of the transient nature of the officers' chosen vocation, locally based insurance agents were often reluctant to insure them and, occasionally, small carriers who provided insurance failed, leaving the officers without insurance. These men, dedicated to serving their nation, decided to serve each other in a novel way. They created an interinsurance exchange called the United States Army Insurance Association. In effect, they pooled their money to insure each other.

From its narrow and humble beginnings, the association of army officers first extended eligibility to officers of the U.S. Navy and the U.S. Marines, and renamed the organization the United Services Automobile Association (USAA) to better reflect its broadened base. Over the years, membership expanded to include all officers—active, separated, retired, reserve, and National Guard. In 1973, USAA extended eligibility for property and casualty insurance to former dependents of military officers. Today, this group is USAA's fastest-growing segment. Most recently, Chairman and CEO retired U.S. Air Force General Robert T. Herres led the effort that culminated in extending USAA membership to the enlisted members of the armed services. The association is now positioned to be the insurance and financial services provider of choice for the entire military community.

Diversification

USAA's drive to become a diversified major financial services company began under the chairmanship of retired U.S. Air Force Brigadier General Robert F. McDermott. Building upon the property and casualty business, and a small life insurance subsidiary, the association added a variety of services and products. These included no-load mutual funds, a discount brokerage service, real estate investments, and a bank with a full line of services, including credit cards. In 1997, USAA served more than 3 million customers—primarily members of the U.S. military and their families. This includes more than 95

Retired U.S. Air Force General Robert T. Herres, chairman and CEO of United Services Automobile Association, led the effort that culminated in extending USAA membership to the enlisted members of the armed services.

percent of all active duty officers. USAA, with owned and managed assets totaling more than $42.7 billion, ranks as the nation's fifth-largest insurer of private passenger automobiles and sixth-largest home owners insurer.

USAA has garnered national awards and honors in recognition of its dedication to service and its distinguished place in America's services sector. In 1993, USAA was listed among the top five companies in the best-selling book *The 100 Best Companies to Work for in America*. Also in 1993, *CIO* magazine listed USAA among the top 21 consumer services as "providing the best infrastructures, applications, and interfaces, and the training and backup to go with them."

In 1995, *Money* rated the USAA Federal Savings Bank as the Best Bank in America. In 1997, *Fortune* ranked USAA 212th out of the 500 largest U.S. corporations in terms of revenues. And, in its March 3, 1997, issue, *Fortune* selected USAA as one of America's Most Admired Companies, and first in the property and casualty industry.

Good Citizen of San Antonio

USAA headquarters is located in northwest San Antonio on a 287-acre campus. Its home office complex provides a very comfortable and efficient work environment for more than 11,500 employees in the city, making USAA San Antonio's largest private employer. An additional 4,100 employees are located at major regional offices in Sacramento, Colorado Springs, Tampa, and Norfolk, Virginia.

In addition to its obvious financial impact on San Antonio's economy, USAA is an outstanding corporate citizen. The USAA Volunteer Corps matches USAA employees with community nonprofit agencies that need additional manpower to achieve their humanitarian goals. In 1996, current and retiree volunteers committed more than 183,000 hours of personal time to more than 350 nonprofit and civic organizations in the community. Almost 1,000 employee volunteers participate in USAA's Community Educational Programs, including one-on-one mentoring and Junior Achievement.

USAA employees are generous with more than their time. They are major participants in donating blood, and, in 1996, USAA employees nationwide contributed $3.6 million to United Way. This was matched by an additional $2 million in corporate funds. Although USAA comprises less than 2 percent of the workforce in San Antonio, USAA's United Way contributions accounted for one out of six dollars donated to the community in 1996.

USAA HEADQUARTERS IS LOCATED IN NORTHWEST SAN ANTONIO ON A **287**-ACRE CAMPUS. ITS HOME OFFICE COMPLEX PROVIDES A VERY COMFORTABLE AND EFFICIENT WORK ENVIRONMENT FOR MORE THAN **11,500** EMPLOYEES IN THE CITY, MAKING **USAA** SAN ANTONIO'S LARGEST PRIVATE EMPLOYER.

GPM Life Insurance Company

When Peter J. Hennessey retired from the U.S. Army in 1929, he planned to offer life insurance to military personnel. In those days, all such policies included a war clause, which limited the amount of payments to survivors of those who died in battle. Hennessey wanted to sell insurance policies without such clauses, but at the time, there were no companies willing to do so. So in May 1934, Hennessey founded Government Personnel Mutual Life Insurance Company, now called GPM Life Insurance Company, in order to offer life insurance to government and military personnel without the exclusionary language.

When Hennessey died suddenly in 1938, his wife, Blanche, assumed the presidency. Although she had no prior business experience, she held the small company together, signing correspondence "B.T. Hennessey" to cloak her gender. She guided the company through World War II, still offering the same benefits to military personnel without the discriminatory war clause. Blanche Hennessey directed the company until 1953, when her son, Peter Hennessey Jr., became president.

Blanche Hennessey continued as the company's board chairwoman until her death at 91 in 1980. Since its inception, the company has been owned by its policyholders, and the Hennessey family continues its management. Peter Hennessey III now serves as president and CEO, and Peter Hennessey Jr. is board chairman.

A History of Success

GPM Life lost some revenues and life insurance in force in the unsettled time following World War II, but the company has earned a profit in 50 of the last 52 years, and insurance in force now totals more than $2.5 billion.

GPM is a midsize company, with about 120 employees locally. Its size permits greater flexibility, and allows it to institute changes in response to policyholder needs faster than larger companies. GPM is licensed in 38 states and the District of Columbia, and maintains a European office. Still primarily a life insurance company for individuals, GPM has broadened its services to include annuities and some group insurance.

Operating from its distinctive twin-tower headquarters at Loop 410 and Blanco Road, GPM Life has returned more than 70 percent of its profits to policyholders since its founding. For many years, GPM's services were primarily for military personnel and their families. Today, military personnel account for about 25 percent of the company's business, and the balance of coverage is extended to civilian and civil service employees.

Continued Growth

In its early years, GPM competed only with smaller companies for military customers. "It was among the first to specialize in military life insurance, and is one of the few remaining," says Peter Hennessey Jr. "We're competing against the giants in the industry now."

The largest area of growth GPM is experiencing today is in the federal civil service sector. GPM's emphasis on policyholder service and recruitment of quality agents, and on setting goals for continuing quality, remains its formula for success.

"Excellent products, superior service, and dedicated agents—it's the name of the game," adds Hennessey. "We have many long-time employees and agents who make the difference—it's a team effort."

Since its inception, GPM Life has been owned by its policyholders, and the Hennessey family continues its management. Peter Hennessey III now serves as president and CEO, and Peter Hennessey Jr. is board chairman (left).

Operating from its distinctive twin-tower headquarters at Loop 410 and Blanco Road, GPM Life has returned more than 70 percent of its profits to policyholders since its founding (right).

Southwest Neon Signs, Inc.

At Southwest Neon Signs, Inc., the final product is more than just an advertising tool. Each customer, from the large corporation to the small family business, gets a custom-designed and professionally crafted sign that carries with it the quality and personal service that have been the hallmark of one of America's premier sign companies for more than 50 years.

American Success Story

More than just providing first-rate products and service, Southwest Neon operates with a professionalism established by its founder Harvey Billingsley. It was two ladders and dedication borne of sweat and life struggles that he loaded into his old Plymouth truck in 1946 to begin the family legacy that is Southwest Neon today. With the philosophy that hard work creates its own good fortune and with the ever present support of his wife, Miss Corinne, the company prospered.

The true character and commitment to excellence exemplified by Harvey was carried forward by next-generation family members assuming key roles in the business. Miss Corinne turned over office operations to daughter Carol Burkett and son Darryl became manager of the company's Austin-area facility in Round Rock. Eldest son Dewayne assumed the principal leadership role at Harvey's semi-retirement in 1980. Gifted in all aspects of business management, guided by an uncompromising sense of honest, fair business practices, and blessed with his parents' love for the sign industry and its people, Dewayne distinguished himself as company president. From 1980 until his death in 1997, Dewayne put Southwest Neon on the cutting edge of sign technology, directing operations such that sales increased from $1 million to more than $11 million annually.

Today, third-generation family members and long-valued company "family" personnel have stepped up to solidify Southwest Neon's place as a sign industry leader for the next century. Growing up in the sign business, Carol's son, Greg Burkett, now serves as company president; her husband and 30-year sign business veteran, Woodrow Burkett, directs a variety of house account operations; her daughter, Sherri Burkett, is service coordinator; and Dewayne's eldest son, Daniel, assists in a variety of computer-related functions.

Innovation and Technology: Signs of the Times

The current San Antonio Southwest Neon facility of more than 90,000 square feet with computer-aided design and fabricating equipment is a far cry from the manufacturing process of Harvey Billingsley's day. While the customer still ranks first in priority, the products and means of creating them are strictly the best the sign industry has to offer. From channel-letters and Plexiglas-faced signs for Ultramar Diamond Shamrock Corporation to mixed-open-faced neon, metal cabinets, and flex-faced sign packages for local entertainment complexes such as Far West Rodeo, Southwest Neon does it all. With other company facilities in Houston, Austin, and Dallas, as well as quality professional affiliates throughout the country, Southwest Neon easily accommodates both one-of-a-kind custom orders and national needs. These run the spectrum from local school marquees and restaurant signs to channel letters and awnings for national companies such as Hollywood Video and Parts America. In addition to state-of-the-art production facilities, Southwest Neon also maintains a fleet of top-notch delivery, installation, and service vehicles manned by experienced, licensed sign technicians.

Much has changed in the sign industry, but the fundamental principles of good business practices exemplified by Harvey and Dewayne Billingsley still are the basis for Southwest Neon today. President Greg Burkett sums it up best: "This business was built on integrity, honesty, and hard work. Our philosophy is: Do what it takes to satisfy the needs of the customer."

With company facilities in San Antonio, Houston, Austin, and Dallas, as well as quality professional affiliates throughout the country, Southwest Neon Signs, Inc. can easily accommodate both one-of-a-kind custom orders and the needs of companies with locations nationwide.

San Antonio Federal Credit Union

San Antonio Federal Credit Union (SACU) got its start from very modest beginnings when a dozen government workers from the old Duncan Field pulled together $60 to form the National Federation of Federal Employees Local 28 Credit Union. In 1935, its first year of operation, the credit union issued 37 loans totaling $1,408.15, and after expenses, the new organization showed a profit of $42.84.

Today, Duncan Field is Kelly Air Force Base and SACU has nearly 251,000 members and 15 branch locations in San Antonio and Houston. With assets of more than $1 billion, it is the 21st-largest credit union in the nation in total assets; the 20th largest in total savings; the seventh largest in total membership; and the 14th largest in total loans.

Changing with the Times

"The reason the credit union was actually started was to generate more members for Local 28. Little did any of us realize what we had started," said Colonel W.C. Strum, who was the group's treasurer in 1935.

By the time Local 28 Credit Union had its first annual meeting in 1936, its membership had grown to 98, including Hortense Seeds, the first woman to be welcomed into the organization. In 1943, Seeds also became the first woman to serve on the board of directors.

The credit union's growth over the years brought many changes to the organization, including several name changes and membership growth—both reflections of the wider net the credit union was throwing into the San Antonio market.

In 1945, the credit union's field of membership was expanded to include other federal workers who were not members of Local 28. By 1952, SACU had reached a milestone of 1,000 members. The credit union's assets reached $1 million in 1959, establishing it as a financial leader in the community. In 1960, SACU was granted permission to open its membership to active military personnel, and 10 years later, it was allowed to accept all retired civil service and military personnel living in San Antonio. By 1972, SACU had become the largest credit union in Texas, with assets totaling more than $50 million. Two years later, total assets had doubled.

SACU continued to grow rapidly during the 1970s and the early 1980s. By the mid-1980s, financial institutions across Texas were experiencing difficulties due to a depression in the oil business and a collapse in real estate values. Many financial institutions failed during this statewide recession, but SACU not only survived, it continued to offer quality products and service to its members. SACU became federally chartered in 1989.

A Billion-Dollar Financial Cooperative

"It amazes me that 12 fellows could join together in 1935 and start a credit union that would grow to more than $1 billion in assets and 251,000 members," says Jeffrey H. Farver, SACU president and CEO. "To me, growth represents the success of any organization. It shows how the members vote with their dollars."

Among its services, SACU offers consumer, education, residential, home equity, vehicle, and credit card loans. The deposit options include checking, share savings, money market, share certificates, and retirement accounts.

The San Antonio Federal Credit Union (SACU) headquarters is located at 6061 IH-10 West at Vance Jackson (left).

Quality member service is part of the "credit union difference." Account service representatives know the importance of providing valuable product and service information to fellow SACU members (right).

Although a credit union offers similar services, it is not a bank. As Farver explains, "We don't try to be a bank. We don't have stockholders; we have members who pool their funds to provide loans to other members. Without stockholders, credit union dividends go to our savers and borrowers. On average, credit union savers get a higher rate on their savings, and borrowers pay lower interest rates on loans."

Over the years, the not-for-profit cooperative has introduced many new services to San Antonio, including share draft accounts, direct deposit, and the first automated teller machines. "Our aim for the future is to have one new full-service SACU branch and 10 new ATMs each year," Farver says. SACU now has more than 100 ATMs in the Greater San Antonio area. The credit union also offers a variety of electronic delivery systems, including Loan Connection™ (loan by phone) and PhoneLink™ (automated telephone service).

Today, SACU's services are accessible and convenient to people in every quadrant of the city. Worldwide, members access credit union information on the SACU Internet home page.

The credit union's membership almost perfectly mirrors the ethnic makeup of San Antonio: approximately 50 percent of the members are Hispanic, 40 percent Anglo-American, 8 percent Afro-American, and 2 percent represent other cultures. The members come from every income level.

People Helping People

Throughout the years, SACU has never veered from the credit union philosophy of People Helping People. "The bottom line is not just dollars and the next financial report. It is human capital and involvement in the community. When the credit union is successful, the community will be successful," Farver says.

Through employee involvement and philanthropy, SACU supports more than 200 People Helping People programs each year, including a low-income housing program with the San Antonio Alternative Housing Corp., Credit Unions for Kids, United Way, Elf Louise, financial seminars for members, Santa Rosa Children's Hospital Tejanos for Children, and Habitat for Humanity.

SACU began the 1990s with renewed direction, with its board of directors, management, and staff united behind the company goal to return to the credit union's roots. With a renewed emphasis on strengthening member relationships and providing excellent member service, SACU is looking toward the future, where it will continue to lead the way in helping people reach their financial goals.

Since 1935, SACU has been a strong community leader. In 1996, a fund was established for the care and restoration of the Alamo that allows SACU members to contribute each time they use an SACU Alamo MasterCard©. Jeffrey H. Farver, president and CEO of SACU, proudly shows his card in front of the historic shrine.

SACU introduced the first automated teller machines (ATMs) to San Antonio in 1975. With more than 100 ATMs in the city today, SACU can provide service to members around the clock (left).

Providing modern branches in all areas of San Antonio is an important part of member service at SACU. The Ingram branch is one of 13 locations in San Antonio (right).

City Public Service

City Public Service (CPS) is one of the nation's largest municipal utilities, serving more than 520,000 electric customers throughout its 1,566-square-mile service area, and about 300,000 natural gas customers in the urban San Antonio area. Forebears of the current utility trace their roots to 1860, when the San Antonio Gas Company began manufacturing and distributing gas for downtown streetlights. The electric business dates back to 1881, three years after Thomas Edison invented the lightbulb.

Purchased in 1942 by the City of San Antonio from investor-owned San Antonio Public Service Co., which operated gas, electric, and bus service in the city, the utility is governed by a five-member board of trustees that includes the mayor. City Public Service returns a percentage of its revenues to the city's general fund each year, and, since its formation, has contributed more than $2 billion to the fund. The $137.6 million CPS payment for the 1996-1997 fiscal year represented the largest source of income for the City of San Antonio and about one-third of the city's general fund.

Reliable Service

City Public Service's goal is to produce reliable, low-cost energy and energy-related services for San Antonio and the surrounding area. Rather than buying its electricity from outside sources, CPS owns and operates two coal-fired and five natural-gas-fired power plants in the San Antonio area, and owns 28 percent of the South Texas Project nuclear plant on the Gulf Coast. The natural gas system has 4,068 miles of lines through which natural gas is delivered to CPS customers.

City Public Service also owns two lakes. Following a severe drought during the early 1950s, Victor Braunig, then general manager of CPS, ordered the utility in 1957 to utilize treated wastewater or sewage effluent for power plant cooling purposes in order to reserve Edwards Aquifer water for drinking purposes. That decision led to the creation of Braunig and Calaveras lakes in southeast Bexar County. The two lakes supply cooling water for four power plants, and offer a source of recreation for fishing, skiing, and camping enthusiasts. The same cooling process is still used today.

Clockwise from top:

Karl Urbankski, Tester III for San Antonio's gas and electric utility, inspects fiber-optic cable on the distribution rack, which serves as a terminal for the glass strands that transfer information among City Public Service facilities.

Calaveras Lake provides wastewater for cooling three City Public Service power plants and offers the community recreational activities, such as fishing and boating.

The utility's Volunteers in Public Service program provides warmth to senior citizens through crocheted shawls and fellowship at a United Way adult day center.

In May 1997, the San Antonio Water System presented CPS with the Pioneer Recycling Award for its water-saving measures. It has been estimated that use of recycled water at the plants has saved more than 171 billion gallons of Edwards Aquifer water, enough to supply the needs of San Antonio for three years.

Low-Cost, Efficient Operations

Efficiency and economy are two hallmarks of CPS operations and service. A fuel diversification program provides for use of coal, natural gas, and nuclear fuel to maintain low fuel costs. Favorable fuel prices, low production costs at its power plants, and sound financial management have enabled CPS to keep its rates the lowest of any major Texas city, and among the lowest in the nation. In 1996-1997, for example, the CPS residential gas and electric bill ranked second lowest among the 20 largest cities in the United States. The utility's consistently favorable bond ratings ensure lower interest rates when CPS requires financing for large projects.

CPS officials work closely with the San Antonio Economic Development Foundation to welcome new industry to the city. "Utilities are very important when you're talking about bringing business to the city," says Barbara Stover, manager of public relations and marketing for CPS. "They want to know that they have a good, reliable source of utility service."

CPS considers its nearly 3,500 employees an essential component to its ongoing commitment to reliable, low-cost service. CPS has a stable workforce, with an average of 14 years of utility experience. The management staff has an average of 22 years of experience in utilities, and is recognized by its peers and acknowledged by the top rating agencies in the country as among the best in the utility industry. A comprehensive training program keeps employees in step with new technology and work processes that help them better serve their customers.

Community Education, Information, Support

CPS also supports the community through education and volunteerism. Free tours and business, civic, and school programs teach participants about the utility, gas and electricity safety, and energy conservation. "Because our business is gas and electric services, we want people to know about them," says Stover. "A big focus is on reaching students with those messages of safety."

Tours of the power plants are eye-opening for visitors, Stover adds. "People are amazed to see what it takes to generate electricity. They flip on the light switch at home, but they have no idea what is behind that."

Residential and business customers also may request a no-cost energy audit. A CPS representative inspects a home or office and leaves a report about energy-saving measures to reduce utility bills.

As a municipal entity, CPS cannot use ratepayer dollars for charitable contributions, but its employees choose each year to give in many ways. "We're proud of our community involvement," says Stover. Under the Volunteers in Public Service program, employees donated 14,055 hours and raised more than $15,000 for nonprofit organizations in 1996-1997. More than 85 percent of the active workforce and 119 CPS retirees contributed to the United Way campaign, which raised $466,345 during that same period. "It means our employees are really community-oriented," says Stover. "They have a real commitment."

The safe, reliable production and delivery of electricity, combined with a sense of responsibility to the community it serves, make City Public Service a vital, driving force in San Antonio.

Expansion of the gas system takes the commodity to growing areas of San Antonio (left).

Coal supplies one-half of CPS electric generation and is a major factor in achieving low production costs (right).

The Dee Howard Co.

After World War II, former U.S. Air Force pilot D.U. "Dee" Howard earned a permanent place in aviation history by recognizing that military aircraft could be converted for use by the rapidly expanding commercial air industry. Howard Aero Inc., the company he founded in 1947 in San Antonio, took the lead in the aircraft retrofitting industry, and has maintained it ever since. Renamed The Dee Howard Co. in 1964, the company now enjoys gross revenues of $100 million a year, and is today known worldwide as a premier modification and maintenance center for commercial aircraft.

"Dee Howard had a typical inventor's mind and the entrepreneurial spirit of a pioneer," says Armando Sassoli, the company's vice president of business development. "He was one of those personalities that was the backbone of the economy of those times."

Innovations for the Jet Age

The Dee Howard Co. occupies a 550,000-square-foot facility on 54 acres at the San Antonio International Airport. Its gigantic hangars can accommodate as many as three Boeing 747s, as well as several narrow-body transports, at the same time. The company employs a growing workforce of more than 1,200, and operates 24 hours a day, seven days a week in order to reduce its customers' downtime and to get aircraft flying again as quickly as possible.

In its early days, the company focused on retrofitting military

The Dee Howard Co.'s gigantic hangars can accommodate as many as three Boeing 747s, as well as several narrow-body transports, at the same time.

The company occupies a 550,000-square-foot facility on 54 acres at the San Antonio International Airport.

aircraft for peacetime use. Today, the focus has changed significantly, according to Sassoli. Now providing an entire range of aircraft maintenance for major airlines and cargo aircraft operators, the company specializes in re-engining and cockpit updating, and designs and manufactures customized parts and tools for even the most sophisticated needs.

When jet aircraft became available to businesses and private owners in the early 1960s, The Dee Howard Co. was ready. Working with Bill Lear Sr., the company created the first three-dimensional mock-up of the Learjet, and has continued to develop significant improvements in the performance, safety, and range of the famous plane.

The Dee Howard Co. has also designed and produced a thrust-reverser device to slow jet aircraft speed during landing. This device has become the world standard for the aerospace industry. "We are the world's leader in the design and manufacture of thrust reversers for business jets," Sassoli says.

The Dee Howard Co. has customized the interior of widebody executive aircraft to accommodate just about every requirement under the sun—from the installation of a complete, state-of-the-art surgical suite to an airborne boardroom and a secure communications center.

QUALITY SERVICE FOR THE FUTURE

In 1990, UPS, the largest package distribution company in the world, was faced with a federal noise-reduction requirement that might have forced it to scrap a fleet of 51 Boeing 727-100s by the year 2000. Instead, UPS commissioned The Dee Howard Co. to replace the original Pratt & Whitney engines in the planes' rugged airframes with new, quieter Rolls-Royce Tay engines. The massive project was turned over to the company's engineering department, which in peak times employs as many as 350 aeronautical engineers. The work set a world record for the largest commercial aircraft modification project.

The project required three years of engineering development and four years' work in the hangar to complete. The last of the re-engined 727-100s, now called 727-QFs, for Quiet Freighters, returned to service at the end of 1996, three years ahead of schedule.

In 1989, The Dee Howard Co. was purchased by Italian aerospace corporation Alenia, a multi-billion-dollar company, and in 1990, after an aviation career spanning 50 years, Howard retired from the business. "Even a great spirit like Dee Howard had to pass the baton," Sassoli says, explaining that technological advances have made aircraft modification more science than art.

Today, The Dee Howard Co. is internationally recognized as a leader in the design and manufacture of thrust reversers and as a first-class facility for the maintenance, modification, and repair of Airbus, ATR, Boeing, and McDonnell Douglas aircraft.

THE DEE HOWARD CO. ENJOYS GROSS REVENUES OF $100 MILLION A YEAR, AND IS KNOWN WORLDWIDE AS A PREMIER MODIFICATION AND MAINTENANCE CENTER FOR COMMERCIAL AIRCRAFT.

Frontier Enterprises

FRONTIER ENTERPRISES, FOUNDED MORE THAN 50 YEARS AGO IN San Antonio by G. "Jim" Hasslocher, is a company whose roots run deep in San Antonio culture. The company operates some of the most popular eating establishments in the city, including Jim's Restaurants, a family favorite for generations and a popular meeting place for businesspeople and prominent political figures.

The company also owns and operates the Magic Time Machine restaurants in San Antonio and Dallas, as well as The Tower Restaurant atop the Tower of the Americas in San Antonio's HemisFair Park. The multimillion-dollar company employs approximately 1,100 people in its restaurants and administrative offices.

Frontier Enterprises has received almost every honor the food service industry has to offer. Hasslocher is a repeated recipient of both the San Antonio and Texas Restaurant Association's Restaurateur of the Year Award, the coveted Gold Plate Award from the International Food Service Manufacturer's Association, the Sara Lee Medallion of Merit, and Florida University's Salut Aux Restaurateurs Award.

Ironically, Hasslocher entered the restaurant business almost by accident. As a young man, his first love was construction. In 1946, upon completing military service, Hasslocher found a deal on 50 army surplus bicycles. He opened a bicycle rental business next to the main entrance to Brackenridge Park and the San Antonio Zoo. In the summer of 1946, he began selling slices of ice-cold watermelon next to the bicycle stand.

Bikes and watermelons soon evolved into hamburgers. Hasslocher's idea of charbroiling

Frontier Enterprises, founded by G. "Jim" Hasslocher, operates some of the most popular eating establishments in San Antonio, including Jim's Restaurants, a family favorite for generations.

In 1973, Frontier Enterprises introduced the Magic Time Machine Restaurant, a fine-dining establishment with costumed characters that delight and entertain their patrons with fun-filled comedy.

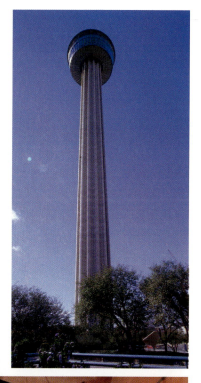

hamburgers quickly became successful. The stand grew into the well-known Frontier Drive-Ins, which became the place where customers ate hamburgers, french fries, and onion rings in their cars, served by Frontier's famous Curbettes (carhops).

A Family Business

From the beginning, Frontier Enterprises has been a family endeavor. The first restaurant opened April 17, 1947, and Jim and Veva Hasslocher were married July 13, 1947. Veva took over the company payroll three days after the marriage and has been working alongside her husband ever since. Today, she is in charge of menu planning, uniforms, decor, office staff, and communications. "I've done just about every job there was to do—except carhop in the drive-in restaurants," she says.

Over time, Frontier Drive-Ins spread throughout San Antonio and became a popular gathering place for young people. Jim's Coffee Shops, which attracted families, politicians, and businesspeople, began its success story in 1963.

Wanting to provide quality products and quality control for

▲ LARRY PEARLSTONE

his restaurants, Hasslocher opened Frontier Meat and Food Service in 1967. The federally inspected meat plant and commissary services all of the Frontier restaurants, as well as hundreds of other food service companies throughout the Southwest. This operation is undergoing expansion to keep pace with its growing business.

Since that time, Frontier Enterprises has expanded to include the sky-high restaurant on top of the Tower of the Americas, which it continues to operate today.

In 1973, the Hasslochers introduced yet another dining experience to Texas—the Magic Time Machine Restaurant, a fine dining establishment with costumed characters that delight and entertain their patrons with fun-filled comedy.

With constant attention to customer satisfaction, the Hasslocher family and Frontier Enterprises are entering their second half-century of serving San Antonio with aggressive growth and renovation plans. It is truly a company with a proud history and a bright future.

CLOCKWISE FROM TOP LEFT: FROM THE BEGINNING, FRONTIER ENTERPRISES HAS BEEN A FAMILY ENDEAVOR. THE FIRST RESTAURANT OPENED APRIL 17, 1947, AND JIM AND VEVA HASSLOCHER WERE MARRIED JULY 13, 1947.

THE TOWER RESTAURANT IS LOCATED ATOP THE TOWER OF THE AMERICAS IN SAN ANTONIO'S HEMISFAIR PARK (LEFT AND TOP RIGHT).

A CULTURAL TAPESTRY

McCombs Enterprises

In January 1958, Red McCombs established a Ford dealership in San Antonio. By 1997, *Automotive News* ranked McCombs Enterprises as the nation's sixth-largest and Texas' number one automobile group, with annual sales of $1.3 billion and 2,000 employees across the state. But McCombs Enterprises is known for more than just its automotive business. Over the years, the company has made its mark on ranching, sports franchises, communications, moviemaking, and many other pursuits.

McCombs Enterprises has a long history in the sports arena. The company was an original investor in the San Antonio Spurs when the basketball team started in 1972. In 1982, the company disposed of its interest in the Spurs and purchased the Denver Nuggets basketball team, which it owned until 1985. In 1988, McCombs again bought the Spurs, but sold the team in 1993, when he was assured that the team would remain in San Antonio.

During the 1980s, in a joint venture with Twentieth Century Fox, the company financed more than 30 movies, including the successful *Romancing the Stone*. McCombs Enterprises also invested in banks and savings and loans, owned a Thoroughbred horse farm in Kentucky, and directed a cattle ranching operation in several states.

In addition to many dealerships across the state of Texas, McCombs Enterprises' automotive interests have included a Subaru import business with a distributorship in Denver. A Kia distributorship, based in Santo Domingo, sent cars to Central and South America and the Caribbean. The company also imported vehicle parts and accessories for General Motors.

How did an automotive dealer become involved in so many industries? "I have been fortunate to access capital," says McCombs, company owner. "I have never had to pass on a business opportunity because of lack of capital." Access to capable associates and a willingness to take risks also have contributed to the company's success.

Current Focus

Currently, McCombs Enterprises owns insurance, finance, and warranty companies to support the automobile dealerships. "We try to have a fully integrated automobile business, where we're performing all of the functions," says Gary Woods, who joined the company

in 1979 and today is president of McCombs Enterprises.

McCombs Enterprises invests in and develops real estate, from raw land and shopping centers to warehouses and office buildings in Houston, San Antonio, and Austin. Its Houston-based oil and gas subsidiary, McCombs Energy, LLC, invests in oil exploration and production, with wells in Texas, Louisiana, and Mississippi. It also has interests in wells and pipelines of other oil and gas companies.

McCombs is the company's representative on the board of directors of Clear Channel Communications, which owns about 200 radio and 15 TV stations, billboard companies, and other broadcast interests worldwide. In 1972, McCombs was one of the original founders of Clear Channel, when the multimedia company was created upon the acquisition of WOAI radio in San Antonio. McCombs is the second-largest shareholder in Clear Channel, which is McCombs Enterprises' largest investment.

McCombs Enterprises is also part owner of Old San Francisco steak houses in San Antonio, Houston, Austin, and Dallas. The company invests in all types of existing companies and ventures that show promise, says Woods, focusing on those that have the greatest potential for return.

Growth and the Community

Although McCombs Enterprises has enjoyed remarkable growth, McCombs admits, "Growth in itself has never been a goal of mine." He credits Woods for much of the company's success. "Since 1979, Gary has been an essential element to our growth and operational activity. He has been since the day he joined me and continues to be today. One of the offshoots of growth is it gives us more resources to participate in community activities."

McCombs Enterprises and the McCombs Foundation, an endowment created in 1981, dedicate funds to support functions that create growth and jobs in the city, and excellence in education and health care. The United Way of San Antonio, the local chambers of commerce, the San Antonio Economic Development Foundation, and colleges and universities are among the entities that receive support.

"There are literally hundreds of activities that we support," says McCombs. "None of this would

Under the leadership of founder Red McCombs, McCombs Enterprises has expanded beyond the automotive industry to include ranching, sports franchises, communications, insurance, finance, real estate, and moviemaking.

be possible without business growth within our companies."

The foundation contributes up to $8 million annually to charities, colleges, and universities across the state. Woods estimates contributions of all sizes go to more than 400 charities each year. A formal program grants scholarships to children of McCombs Enterprises employees.

Looking to the Future

McCombs Enterprises can point to success in many areas, but McCombs considers the company's biggest accomplishment to be the effect it has had on its employees. "Our biggest achievement? Being able to grow in size and provide jobs that train people for even better jobs." The automotive division, for example, has trained and offered financial assistance to employees, about 50 of whom are now auto dealers themselves.

The future holds more of the same for the company, says Woods. Although its enterprises seem unrelated, there is a common thread, he adds. "We try to get the best managers and the best employees we can get. We instill a sense of loyalty and ownership, and let people perform. We will continue to invest in good people."

Says McCombs, "Every day we look for other business opportunities, never knowing what or where or when. There is no plan." But there is a tradition of success that McCombs Enterprises is sure to continue for many years to come.

IN 1997, *AUTOMOTIVE NEWS* RANKED MCCOMBS ENTERPRISES AS THE NATION'S SIXTH-LARGEST AND TEXAS' NUMBER ONE AUTOMOBILE GROUP, WITH ANNUAL SALES OF $1.3 BILLION AND 2,000 EMPLOYEES ACROSS THE STATE.

A CULTURAL TAPESTRY

University of Texas Health Science Center at San Antonio

When the Texas legislature chartered the South Texas Medical School in 1959, few would have predicted that it would become one of the nation's leading university research centers in such a short time. The University of Texas Health Science Center at San Antonio (UTHSC) became a full-fledged health science center in 1972, and has been making strides in education, research, patient care, and community service ever since. The school that broke ground in an outlying suburb of San Antonio has helped spawn an entire medical center complex, and has contributed to one of the city's top industries—the biosciences—with an estimated impact of approximately $1 billion annually on the San Antonio economy.

As a state, national, and international leader in the biosciences for its innovative teaching and major research breakthroughs, UTHSC is one of 15 components in the University of Texas System. Its five schools—medical, dental, nursing, allied health sciences, and graduate school of biomedical sciences—annually enroll more than 2,700 students in more than 20 degree and certificate programs.

Research and Training

Innovative and visionary, the Health Science Center provides an environment in which scientists conduct major studies in diabetes, aging, cancer, AIDS, stroke prevention, and other fields, while expanding the knowledge of basic biomedical sciences and contributing to the development of new drugs. The Health Science Center's Institute of Biotechnology conducts genetics research, and a state-of-the-art Research Imaging Center supports research and education and is an international leader in mapping the human brain.

UTHSC is one of 16 sites in the world approved by the National Cancer Institute for patient trials of new anticancer drugs. Its transplantation program has one of the highest success rates in the nation. The university's dental school has consistently been ranked number one in the nation by *U.S. News & World Report* and ranks among the nation's highest echelons in dental research nationwide. The Institute for Scientific Information ranks UTHSC ninth in the United States for frequency of citations for its research by colleagues worldwide.

Mission of Service

UTHSC's mission is fourfold: health education, research, patient care, and community service. The center provides health education for all of South Texas, a regional responsibility it takes seriously. From site visits in underserved areas of South Texas to its traveling dental care van and health fairs, UTHSC shares its vast knowledge and resources throughout the region.

Students gain clinical experience and training under faculty supervision at University Hospital, the Audie Murphy Division of South Texas Veterans Health Care System, University Health Center-Downtown, and many other affiliated hospitals, clinics, and related community institutions. The Health Science Center delivers about $50 million in donated care for the medically indigent each year.

UTHSC continues to grow under John P. Howe III, M.D., who has been president and chief executive officer since 1984. In 1998, research dollars to the center had grown to $110 million, and the endowment has more than doubled since 1989. With its steady growth and history of achievement, UTHSC stands ready to fulfill its mission in San Antonio, in Texas, and in the nation.

Innovative and visionary, the University of Texas Health Science Center at San Antonio (UTHSC) provides an environment in which scientists conduct major studies in diabetes, aging, cancer, AIDS, stroke prevention, and other fields, while expanding the knowledge of basic biomedical sciences and contributing to the development of new drugs (top).

The Health Science Center was established in 1972 and has been making strides in education, research, patient care, and community service ever since (bottom).

1965 - 1997

1965   Pape-Dawson Engineers, Inc.

1965   Waterman Broadcasting Corporation of Texas

1968   Datapoint Corporation

1976   Kinetic Concepts, Inc.

1976   Southwest Business Corporation

1979   The Domestic Agency

1980   Valero Energy Corporation

1982   Bradfield Properties Realtors

1985   Bay Networks

1985   MMI, Inc.

1986   Coldwell Banker D'Ann Harper, REALTORS

1987   Ultramar Diamond Shamrock Corporation

1988   HEALTHSOUTH Rehabilitation Institute of San Antonio (RIOSA)

1988   Vencor Hospital-San Antonio

1989   Phyllis Browning Company

1989   Warm Springs Rehabilitation System

1990   Sony Semiconductor Company of America

1993   Euro-Alamo Management, Inc.

1993   SBC Communications Inc.

1997   PG&E Gas Transmission, Texas Corporation

Pape-Dawson Engineers, Inc.

The year was 1965. San Antonio was known mostly for its history and military bases, while a Texan, Lyndon Baines Johnson, occupied the White House. It was also the year that Gus Pape and Gene Dawson Sr. realized the potential of the city and started a new company. A small office was rented and work was begun on surveying and civil engineering projects.

From humble beginnings, Pape-Dawson Engineers, Inc. has emerged as one of the largest and most diversified locally owned engineering companies in south Texas. The company has a staff of 150 and operates within eight technical areas. In 1997, *Engineering News Record* recognized Pape-Dawson as one of the 500 largest design firms in the nation. Pape has since retired, but Gene Dawson continues to serve as chairman of the board.

Formula for Success

The formula for Pape-Dawson's success is contained in the company's mission statement. A commitment to quality, the hiring of innovative engineers, and the offering of solutions that serve the best interests of the client and the public are principles that have guided the firm throughout its history. For employees, the company stresses a sharpening of technical skills, active participation in civic and professional associations, and, above all, character and moral integrity.

Pape-Dawson's staff reflects the cosmopolitan nature of San Antonio. Some 60 percent are minorities and women. The majority have professional registrations, and many have been recognized for achievement. Pape-Dawson believes that retaining quality employees fosters an atmosphere for new ideas and technologies.

Pape-Dawson's early focus was to provide service. No matter if the client was a contractor or a rancher, Pape-Dawson established a reputation for providing the necessary skills in a timely manner. Pape-Dawson also became known for helping with civic and community activities.

In the early 1970s, the economic health of San Antonio was in peril due to the lack of wastewater treatment facilities. The need for a master plan became apparent, and Pape-Dawson was quick to mobilize and tackle the problem. With Pape-Dawson leading a consortium of prominent firms, federal funds were granted, a management plan was developed, sewer lines were installed, and a new treatment plant was built.

During the 1980s, San Antonio blossomed as a tourist destination. Sea World and Fiesta Texas were announced as theme parks, and Pape-Dawson played a significant role for each.

For Sea World, infrastructure, pedestrian walkways, lakes, drainage, and utilities were designed, along with a saltwater recirculation system for the marine animals. For Fiesta Texas, the challenge was to prepare a plan to transform a former quarry into a family-oriented theme park. Undaunted, Pape-Dawson's engineers helped develop a plan that transformed the area into a park featuring amusement rides, cultural exhibits, and musical shows. A unique shaft and tunnel design was provided for a railroad train ride, along with drainage plans and a water treatment system.

Pape-Dawson's new corporate headquarters was designed and built to accommodate the future demands of the engineering, environmental, and surveying professions while at the same time maintaining an architecture to reflect the character of the region.

Pape-Dawson's success in the 1990s resulted from its reputation for quality, coupled with regional growth. Transportation, corporate expansions, new industries, redevelopment, and housing became dominant themes, with Pape-Dawson on the cutting edge of each.

Pape-Dawson was chosen by the City of San Antonio to provide planning and engineering for the Wurzbach Parkway, and was also selected as part of a design team to prepare plans for the complex IH 410/US 281 intersection.

Due to the favorable climate, ideal living conditions, and neighborly treatment of businesses, San Antonio has been fortunate to attract new businesses and foster corporate expansions. Pape-Dawson is providing services to firms such as Citicorp, USAA, Capital Group, Ultramar Diamond Shamrock, Valero Energy, and WorldCom. New industries that Pape-Dawson has assisted include World Savings and Loan and the biotechnology-oriented Texas Research Park.

As the need for housing has grown, tracts of abandoned industrial lands with favorable locations have become valuable for redevelopment. Working with the private sector, Pape-Dawson has promoted plans resulting in the transformation of these lands into golf courses, shopping malls, and residential areas. Examples include LaCantera Golf Course, Lincoln Heights, Quarry Golf Course, and Alamo Quarry Market Place.

Pape-Dawson is also well known for the creation of outstanding residential areas such as Elm Creek, Oakwell Farms, Dominion, Crownridge, Vineyards, and Rogers Ranch, and for resort design for the Hyatt Hill Country and LaCantera.

GROWTH AREAS

Pape-Dawson is currently expanding services to the United States/Mexico border area, while enhancing its water-recycling and environmental capabilities. Work along the border includes design of a designated truck route that will connect to a new international bridge, and provision of engineering services for wastewater treatment plants.

Water issues continue to be paramount in the Southwest. Pape-Dawson is leading a group of companies in designing and constructing a water-recycling system for the San Antonio Water System, which will recycle some 35,000 acre-feet of nonpotable water for industry and agriculture.

PAPE-DAWSON TODAY

Pape-Dawson looks forward to the 21st century with optimism. The leadership of the company has been delegated to Gene Dawson Jr. and Sam Dawson. Continuing with tradition, many of the officers serve on boards and committees for civic and professional organizations. Today, Pape-Dawson's areas of technical expertise include public works, transportation, industry, land development, recreation, the environment, geosciences, and surveying.

Over the past 33 years, Pape-Dawson has evolved from a fledgling enterprise into a recognized leader. The services offered are fulfilled through a cultural tapestry of dedicated, hardworking employees. Guided by its principles and galvanized by a reputation for quality, integrity, and commitment to the community, Pape-Dawson is poised for future challenges, and is certain to be a positive force for years to come.

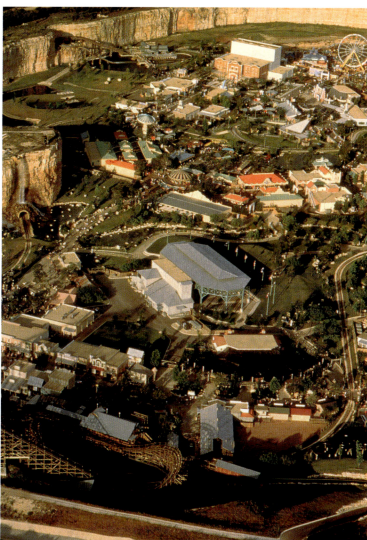

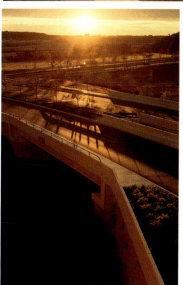

CLOCKWISE FROM TOP LEFT:
LAND DEVELOPMENT AND MASTER-PLANNING SERVICES PROVIDED BY PAPE-DAWSON BLEND TOGETHER THE UNIQUE SCENERY, NATURAL RESOURCES, AND CULTURAL HERITAGE OF THE AREA.

THEME PARKS SUCH AS SIX FLAGS' FIESTA TEXAS REPRESENT A VIBRANT RECREATIONAL MARKET SECTOR POISED FOR CONTINUED GROWTH. PAPE-DAWSON PROVIDED THE CIVIL DESIGN FOR THIS INNOVATIVE PARK, WHICH IS LOCATED ON THE SITE OF A FORMER QUARRY.

PUBLIC WORKS AND TRANSPORTATION PROJECTS INCLUDING HIGHWAYS, STREETS, DRAINAGES, WATER TREATMENT PLANTS, AND UTILITY CONVEYANCES CONTINUE TO BE A MAJOR PORTION OF PAPE-DAWSON'S AGENDA AS THE AREA PROSPERS AND GROWS.

Waterman Broadcasting Corporation of Texas

Owned since 1965 by Waterman Broadcasting Corporation of Texas, KTSA Radio currently has the longest continuous ownership of any broadcast medium in San Antonio. KTSA's owner has resisted selling out to the conglomerates that control most of the other airwave outlets for one reason: Bernard E. Waterman, president of the company, loves the broadcasting business.

"Mr. Waterman started out in broadcast sports, doing play-by-play, and he has preferred to stay in the business," says Joe Ernest, vice president and general manager of KTSA and its sister station, KTFM. Waterman moved to the other side of the microphone in the 1950s, when he purchased station WAAB in Worcester, Massachusetts. Since then, his company has acquired television stations WVIR in Virginia, and WBBH and WZVN in Florida.

A San Antonio Tradition

KTSA, Texas' third-oldest continuously licensed AM broadcast station, is an ABC affiliate that mixes coverage of national news and local talk with spot-news coverage. Its news-based talk format offers callers an opportunity to sound off about events of the day. Rush Limbaugh and Dr. Laura Schlessinger headline the station's slate of talk shows, which is rounded out by local hosts Ricci and Trey Ware, Brad Messer, Eliza Sonneland, Carl Wiglesworth, and Michael O'Rourke.

"It's like an old-fashioned town hall meeting," says Ernest. "People can call in and discuss issues that are going on now."

Waterman Broadcasting launched KTFM in 1968. KTFM, whose broadcast product is a fixture in many thousands of San Antonio homes, vehicles, and offices, features contemporary dance music.

A Commitment to the Community

KTSA and KTFM are heavily involved in community affairs, sponsoring many recurring campaigns. One example is Project Corazon, a drive to encourage donations to the South Texas Blood and Tissue Center. Shots for Tots, a drive to promote the health and safety of youngsters in the San Antonio area, pays for immunizations against childhood diseases.

An annual, three-day South Texas Health and Medicine Expo, sponsored by Waterman Broadcasting in cooperation with the University of Texas Health Science Center at San Antonio, Brooke Army Medical Center at Fort Sam Houston, and Wilford Hall Medical Center at Lackland AFB, has an ongoing impact on the well-being of people in the community.

One of Waterman Broadcasting's most community-enriching efforts began with a 1983 campaign to light up the San Antonio River Walk for the holiday season. In partnership with the Paseo del Rio Association, the company started the Holiday River Parade and the annual lighting that transforms the River Walk into a Christmas wonderland, enchanting local residents and attracting tourists throughout the country. Adding to the charm of the holidays is A Little Christmas Village at LaVillita, a monthlong celebration of Christmas in the historic district and a new tradition for San Antonio families.

"We've been here so long, we're really in tune with the community," says Ernest. "Throughout the period of Waterman's ownership, we have been major contributors to the community. Our emphasis on community involvement is our continuing legacy."

Waterman Broadcasting plays an active role in the community, helping to sponsor many campaigns and projects that enrich the lives of San Antonians. One such project is the annual three-day South Texas Health and Medicine Expo (bottom); in another partnership, Waterman started the Holiday River Parade, which has added the new tradition of A Little Christmas Village at LaVillita, shown in this painting by Thom Ricks (top).

Datapoint Corporation

ANYONE WHO WORKS AT A DESKTOP PC IS USING TECHnology that started at Datapoint Corporation. In business since 1968, Datapoint boasts a list of firsts that revolutionized the way the world works and the way people communicate. Datapoint developed the first microchip that made it possible to produce the first desktop PC. "We are a company known for technological innovation," says Michael Black, vice president of U.S. sales and marketing. "We put the first personal computer on the desktop." The company's engineers invented local area networking, created the first client/server architecture, and designed the first multispeed LAN and the first multiprocessor system that uses INTEL technology.

A Company of Firsts

A leader in telephony, Datapoint was among the first to create an intelligent telephone switching network, or private branch exchange (PBX), which allowed companies to create in-house telephone systems that process calls independent of the local telephone company. Datapoint also developed video PBX technology, which brings a videographic capability to the switching system. Although the videoconferencing technology is only now joining the mainstream, the company was the first to introduce video teleconferencing for the desktop in 1985.

Today, Datapoint focuses its R&D and engineering efforts in three main areas: telephony, data and application servers, and videoconferencing. "We have significant patented technologies in all three areas," says Black. "Patentable technology is a continuing goal." Datapoint's clients primarily are from the commercial and local, state, and federal government sectors.

Worldwide, Datapoint has approximately 700 employees. The company, in conjunction with subsidiaries and distributors, has sales and service operations in 40 countries. A large portion of Datapoint's business is conducted outside the United States. Its U.S. headquarters is in San Antonio, and the company's international headquarters is in Paris. The R&D, engineering, and corporate financial groups, plus the manufacturing, production, and shipping departments, are based in San Antonio. "Regardless of location, Datapoint's strength is in developing technology and putting it to work for our customers," says Black.

Making Technology Work

"We work with clients to make sure the technology does what they want it to do," says Black. "They can count on us. That working relationship is what made us successful, and it's what keeps us successful today."

The company continues to focus on developing new technologies in telephony, video and data communications, and client/server applications. "We've had success in these fields, we have the expertise, and it continues to be our focus," says Black.

Datapoint, indeed, has had an impact on the world of high technology, and has paved the way for other companies of its type to be established in San Antonio. Now entering its 30th year in business, the company is an elder statesman in the field of high technology, and continues to provide technological leadership in the industry.

CLOCKWISE FROM TOP: DATAPOINT CORPORATION'S U.S. HEADQUARTERS IS IN SAN ANTONIO. WITH APPROXIMATELY 700 EMPLOYEES WORLDWIDE, DATAPOINT HAS SALES AND SERVICE OPERATIONS IN 40 COUNTRIES.

TODAY, DATAPOINT FOCUSES ITS R&D AND ENGINEERING EFFORTS IN THREE MAIN AREAS: TELEPHONY, DATA AND APPLICATION SERVERS, AND VIDEOCONFERENCING.

DATAPOINT WAS AMONG THE FIRST TO CREATE AN INTELLIGENT TELEPHONE SWITCHING NETWORK, AND DEVELOPED VIDEO PBX TECHNOLOGY.

Kinetic Concepts, Inc.

Kinetic Concepts, Inc. (KCI) is the realization of one emergency room physician's goal: to prevent the life-threatening complications that arise from immobility due to illness or injury. To this end, the company offers a broad range of innovative healing systems that have saved countless lives in trauma centers and emergency rooms around the world.

KCI started with just one product. James R. Leininger, M.D., KCI founder and chairman emeritus, saw emergency room patients survive serious trauma, then develop life-threatening conditions because they were immobilized. To prevent this, Leininger purchased the rights to market a rotating hospital bed, the Roto Rest, that could prevent fluid buildup in the lungs by rotating laterally to each side.

Seeing an immediate need for this product in the medical community, Leininger revolutionized the health care industry by offering the Roto Rest for rent, a cost-effective alternative that gave facilities access to an important therapy without a corresponding major capital outlay. Today, KCI's business is 90 percent rental. Company representatives deliver the specialty beds, place patients on them, visit to check patient progress, and handle all maintenance and repair requests. This allows hospitals to quickly respond to patient needs, without going through all the red tape of buying a new bed. "With rare exception, we can get to any hospital within two hours and place a patient on our bed, 24 hours a day, seven days a week," says Leininger.

A Continuing Need

KCI remained a single-product company from its beginning until 1985, when it realized that there were additional needs that the company could address. KCI has since moved from offering one type of bed to global marketing of specialty beds, mattress replacement systems, and related medical devices that address skin breakdown, circulatory complications, and pulmonary problems associated with immobility.

KCI has also developed a line of pressure-reducing support surfaces, from hospital mattresses that reduce skin pressure to beds that alternate pressure up and down the body. Burn patients, diabetics, the elderly, and people with swelling or edema benefit from using such products.

Another focus is bariatrics, or products for the obese. "More than 600,000 hospital admissions each year have a primary or secondary diagnosis of obesity," says Leininger. KCI's BariKare bed converts to a chair, with multiple positions in between, so obese patients literally can walk out of their beds. Associated specialized medical equipment, including wheelchairs and walkers, is also offered.

KCI also markets two devices that alleviate other complications that often arise as a result of immobility. Its PlexiPulse enhances blood

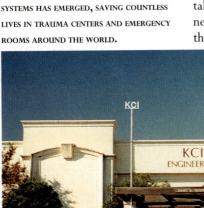

Clockwise from top:

The KCI Tower, home of Kinetic Concepts, Inc.'s corporate headquarters, graces the skyline of northwest San Antonio.

At KCI's manufacturing facility, employees make products used to help prevent complications that arise from the immobility of hospital patients.

From KCI's engineering facility, a broad range of innovative healing systems has emerged, saving countless lives in trauma centers and emergency rooms around the world.

flow, eliminating venous stasis and preventing clotting. Postoperative patients, particularly orthopedic patients, use PlexiPulse. The Wound VAC applies mild suction to pressure ulcers and other chronic wounds to remove excess fluid and bacteria, and increase blood supply. Studies show more than 2.8 million patients suffer from chronic wounds.

This extensive line of products serves hundreds of thousands of patients each year, earning the company more than $300 million in sales in 1996.

People with Purpose

KCI has five locations in San Antonio, including its corporate headquarters, and 144 service centers nationwide, with more than 2,100 employees worldwide. Its motto, People with Purpose, is born out of the services it provides and its internal policies.

KCI, most of all, is a company with a heart, says Leininger. "It's not just a business; it's how we develop personal, caring relationships with our customers and how we treat employees." The company places a strong emphasis on integrity, leadership, and teamwork, letting its employees know their company will assist them in times of crisis.

KCI also reaches out to the community. KCI supports Special Olympics with both time and money; about 100 employees volunteer to work at the annual Spring Games for South Texas, and the company funds the postgame victory dance for the approximately 500 athletes and their families. Medical causes and children's charities, including the Children's Habilitation Center, also receive assistance from KCI. Last year, more than 400 reconditioned KCI beds were donated to hospitals in third world countries.

Looking toward the future, not only will KCI continue to offer its present line of products, but the company will also examine associated technologies and companies to extend its product lines and devise innovative techniques. "We're looking everywhere for new ideas," says Leininger. But above all, Leininger is most proud of his company's industry-changing innovations, noting, "We introduced new therapies and changed the way medicine was practiced in dealing with immobilized patients and their complications." And KCI plans to continue this tradition of more than 20 years of success and innovation in health care treatments.

THE FIRST BARIAIR PRODUCTS ROLL OFF THE ASSEMBLY LINE (TOP).

A KCI TEAM MEMBER MAKES ADJUSTMENTS ON ONE OF KCI'S NEWEST PRODUCTS, THE PEDIDYNE (BOTTOM).

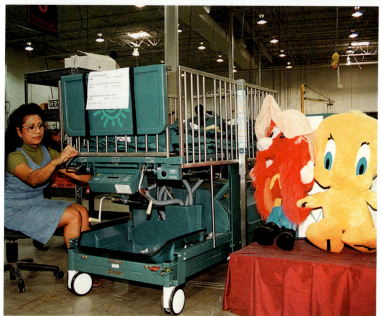

Southwest Business Corporation

CHARLES AMATO AND GARY DUDLEY, GRADE SCHOOL friends who met again in college, began Southwest Business Corporation (SWBC) in 1976 to provide insurance and financial services for lending institutions. Beginning with just three employees, Amato and Dudley have built SWBC into a complete insurance and financial services company with more than 300 employees, offices in seven states, and annual gross revenues approaching $200 million.

Although SWBC historically provided insurance and financial services to financial institutions, today it has expanded to include a wide range of mortgage loan, retail insurance, and investment products and services. This pattern of success has led to expanding SWBC's operations overseas. The San Antonio-based company has met the stringent requirements of the Lloyds of London Tribunal to qualify to represent this organization, and has an interest in a Lloyds correspondent brokerage firm in London. Through that affiliation, SWBC clients who require solutions for complex risk challenges enjoy the significant advantage of tailored insurance programs that meet their unique objectives.

By successfully meeting its clients' needs, SWBC continues to grow. "Charlie and I have always had a philosophy that in order to succeed in the long term, we had to diversify our products and our geographic scope," says Dudley. "Listening to our clients, identifying their needs, and satisfying their objectives within our capabilities and focus has built one successful partnership after another. We're not everything to everyone, but what we do, we do well," he adds.

CONSISTENT SERVICE
Yet despite this growth, some things haven't changed. "Our longtime clients applaud our success, but always say that our work style hasn't changed," notes Dudley.

"We take time to get to know our clients," adds Amato. "We have more than a product relationship, we have a partnership with our clients. We recognize the challenges they face in everyday business and strive to proactively complement their efforts through our strategic alliance."

"We are committed to continuous improvement of technology to ensure the most efficient delivery of client products and services," says Dudley. The company consistently reinvests a large percentage of its earnings to reinforce this substantial aspect of SWBC's corporate strategy. "Our clients have

GARY DUDLEY (LEFT) AND CHARLES AMATO FOUNDED SOUTHWEST BUSINESS CORPORATION (SWBC) IN 1976 TO PROVIDE INSURANCE AND FINANCIAL SERVICES FOR LENDING INSTITUTIONS.

THE ABILITY TO STAY ON THE LEADING EDGE OF TECHNOLOGY WHILE STILL OFFERING FRIENDLY, PERSONAL SERVICE IS WHAT SETS SWBC APART.

become more sophisticated over the years, and we must keep up while maintaining a balance between personal service and technology," he stresses.

The ability to stay on the leading edge of technology while still offering friendly, personal service is what sets SWBC apart. The company culture is often cause for compliments, the cofounders say. When prospective clients visit, they almost always comment on the energy, enthusiasm, and friendliness of the employees. "It's a family, and we've maintained that even though we now have more than 300 employees," says Amato.

Adds Dudley, "We take the same personal interest in our team of professionals as we do with our clients. We take care of our employees. They are our strength, and while they don't appear on the balance sheet, the people of SWBC are our most important asset. People here know if they're in a jam, we'll help them."

GIVING BACK

This attitude of support extends to the San Antonio community. Dudley serves on the development board for the University of the Incarnate Word and worked with the 1997 Rey Feo to raise funds for scholarships for the League of United Latin American Citizens. Amato serves on boards for the Santa Rosa Health System, University of Texas at San Antonio, Junior Achievement, and San Antonio Spurs Foundation.

SWBC is also a minority owner of the San Antonio Spurs, and is active in many local business associations and charities whose main focus is children. SWBC cofounded Credit Unions for Kids and is a leading supporter of Children's Miracle Network. Amato serves on its national board of trustees.

In 1993, SWBC created Take Stock in San Antonio, an annual event at which investors are offered the opportunity to purchase commission-free stock in locally based public companies. In 1997, when Take Stock offered free trades, more than 2,000 prospective buyers attended.

"We started Take Stock in San Antonio to help the community become aware of publicly traded companies and to encourage support for them," says Amato. "They're the companies that help keep the city growing and make it an attractive place to live.

"The city of San Antonio has been good to us, and we feel it's a partnership," says Amato. "As a company, we are very pleased to give back to the community and look forward to expanding this philosophy of giving back as we continue to grow nationally."

"WE ARE COMMITTED TO CONTINUOUS IMPROVEMENT OF TECHNOLOGY TO ENSURE THE MOST EFFICIENT DELIVERY OF CLIENT PRODUCTS AND SERVICES," SAYS DUDLEY.

SWBC HAS GROWN INTO A COMPLETE INSURANCE AND FINANCIAL SERVICES COMPANY, WITH MORE THAN 300 EMPLOYEES AND OFFICES IN SEVEN STATES (LEFT).

SWBC IS A MINORITY OWNER OF THE SAN ANTONIO SPURS, AND IS ALSO ACTIVE IN MANY LOCAL BUSINESS ASSOCIATIONS AND CHARITIES (RIGHT).

The Domestic Agency

FINDING QUALITY CHILD CARE IS A NECESSITY FOR THOUSANDS of working parents across America. In the late seventies, Hope Andrade and Claire Guarnero-Flores, two San Antonians who traveled for business, were concerned about the quality of in-home child care available in their absence. Frustrated by the lack of choices available to them, Andrade and Guarnero-Flores decided to do something about it.

"I looked for help, but found there wasn't anybody who could help me," says Andrade. "We wondered how many other people were faced with this." In 1979, while still employed by other companies, the two placed an advertisement offering domestic help, and hired an answering service. "The phone started ringing," says Andrade.

Fulfilling a Need

Within eight months after placing their initial advertisement, Andrade and Guarnero-Flores left their own jobs to meet the growing demands of their new business, which they named the Domestic Agency. The company initially provided full-time housekeepers, child care, handymen, and chauffeurs to the affluent, but as more working professionals inquired about child care, its focus shifted. Today, the Domestic Agency specializes in child care and care for the elderly, offering full-time support personnel to more than 300 clients annually in the San Antonio area. In 1996, OptimaCare, a home health care agency, was added to offer additional services for the elderly.

In the beginning, the Domestic Agency provided temporary domestic workers only. But many clients were so pleased with the agency's selection of employees and its careful attention to placement needs that they requested full-time placement of personnel. Customer service, Andrade says, is the key to the Domestic Agency's success. "We listen to what the client needs and take time to match the appropriate person with them," she says. "We really care about every one of our clients who calls in."

Being provided with reliable in-home child care and related services creates a sense of security for clients of the Domestic Agency. "Clients are comforted, knowing that we'll be here tomorrow," says Andrade.

Customer satisfaction leads to vital word-of-mouth advertising for the Domestic Agency. Andrade also points with pride to the many long-term relationships her agency has helped establish. Some nannies, for example, have worked for the same families for 10 years. Citing good employees as an essential element, she says, "We can sell the business, but our employees deliver the service."

The Domestic Agency was so successful in San Antonio that Andrade and Guarnero-Flores opened a Dallas office in 1996, and will expand into Houston in 1998. The company's growth is testimony to the quality service provided by the Domestic Agency to its clients, and it is a tradition that Andrade and Guarnero-Flores will continue for many years to come.

The Domestic Agency was founded by Hope Andrade (left) and Claire Guarnero-Flores, and today specializes in child care and care for the elderly.

VALERO ENERGY CORPORATION

VALERO ENERGY CORPORATION WAS CREATED IN 1980 AS the result of a settlement approved by the Texas Railroad Commission, the state's natural gas regulatory agency. Its formation brought an end to nearly seven years of litigation against Coastal States Gas Corporation by municipal natural gas customers; at the time, it was the largest corporate spin-off in U.S. history.

Like its namesake, Mission San Antonio de Valero, the original name of the Alamo, Valero Energy has faced many challenges. Defenders of the Alamo saw defeat; but Valero, under the direction of Chairman and CEO Bill Greehey, has achieved success.

FROM CHALLENGES TO SUCCESS

Although its beginnings were in the natural gas industry, Valero quickly expanded into other areas of the energy sector. In 1981, Valero acquired an interest in a small crude refining operation in Corpus Christi. Envisioning growing worldwide environmental concerns, Valero invested $600 million in the facility and, in 1984, placed into service a state-of-the-art refinery specializing in the production of clean-burning fuels.

International fluctuations in the industry during the mid-1980s brought hard times to Valero. In 1986, the company reported a $100 million loss, but swiftly recovered, and, by 1990, reported net income of $95 million. In 1996, Valero Energy's total assets were reported at $3.2 billion.

Today, Valero Energy is one of the five largest independent refiners and marketers in the nation, and the largest on the Gulf Coast. In 1997, Valero Energy entered into a $1.5 billion agreement with PG&E Corp. to merge its natural gas business with a subsidiary of PG&E. As part of the transaction, Valero spun off its wholly owned subsidiary, Valero Refining and Marketing Company, as an independent, publicly traded company, which retained the name Valero Energy Corporation. With the acquisition of Basis Petroleum, Inc., that same year, Valero Energy now owns and operates four refineries in Texas and Louisiana, with a combined throughput capacity of more than 500,000 barrels per day.

ENVIRONMENTAL STEWARDSHIP

Valero Energy is recognized as an industry leader in the production of premium, environmentally clean products. In 1995, the company received the Texas Governor's Award for Environmental Excellence in recognition of its voluntary efforts to provide a cleaner environment. Valero received the 1996 Environmental Leadership Award from *Hart's Fuel and Technology Management* magazine for outstanding environmental stewardship and leadership.

Valero Energy's commitment to improving the quality of life in communities where it has operations is as old as the company itself. Each year, Valero allocates a percentage of its income to charitable contributions. In 1996, the company gave $1.3 million to nonprofit organizations and community activities. Additionally, Valero employees have devoted many hours of their own time to good causes throughout the city.

In 1993, Valero Energy became the smallest company ever to receive the Spirit of America award, the United Way's highest national corporate honor. Valero's per capita United Way gift in San Antonio reached $995 in 1997.

"At Valero, we have a philosophy that when your employees care about the community and about other people, they will care more about their job, the company, and their fellow employees, and as a result, the company will be more successful," says Greehey. It is a philosophy well proved by the continuing growth and success of Valero Energy Corporation.

VALERO ENERGY CORPORATION'S STATE-OF-THE-ART REFINERY IN CORPUS CHRISTI PRODUCES CLEAN-BURNING FUELS SUCH AS REFORMULATED GASOLINE AND LOW-SULFUR DIESEL (LEFT).

VALERO'S EMPLOYEES ARE ACTIVELY INVOLVED IN THEIR COMMUNITIES THROUGH PROJECTS SUCH AS STUDENT MENTORING AT FREDERICK DOUGLASS INTERMEDIATE LEARNING CENTER (RIGHT).

Bradfield Properties Realtors

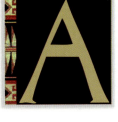

A FULL-SERVICE REAL ESTATE COMPANY WITH MORE THAN 200 Realtors and 56 employees working in seven offices, Bradfield Properties Realtors serves all areas of San Antonio and the surrounding counties, including Boerne, New Braunfels, and the Hill Country. In 1997, Bradfield Properties was ranked as the city's largest residential real estate brokerage firm by the *San Antonio Business Journal*, with sales of $313 million.

Under the direction of Joyce and Boyd Bradfield, who founded the company in 1982, Bradfield Properties has grown from residential sales to include new home marketing and sales, property management, leasing, relocation, commercial sales and business brokerage, title agency, and mortgage divisions. Still, the firm has never lost its personal touch, offering one-to-one service to each and every client.

Personal Service

That one-to-one service is the reason for its success, says Boyd Bradfield, president of Bradfield Properties. "We remain involved in the day-to-day operations of the company: Joyce still answers her own phone and I am always available to anyone in the company," says Bradfield. "It's not a job to them; it's their life—24 hours a day, seven days a week," adds the Bradfields' daughter Kristy Bradfield Petlin, vice president of marketing/advertising.

A San Antonio native, Joyce began her real estate career in 1980. Initially operating out of two offices, Bradfield Properties added locations around the city as demand for the company's services increased. The Bradfields added REAL Mortgage, Apartment Finders, and the commercial real estate divisions as the need arose. Other divisions include New Homes, Relocation, and Property Management, as well as a partnership with Ticor Title Agency.

"The more the company grew, the more requests our Realtors got for other home-related services," says Petlin. Operating under its motto, "We'll get you home," Bradfield Properties combines its many enterprises to fulfill its goal of being a true one-stop shop for all real estate needs.

Alliances for Total Service

In 1997, the company entered into an alliance with Scobey Moving. Plans for similar alliances with home security agencies, swimming pool companies, and other businesses related to complete service for the home are under way. In addition, Bradfield Properties is increasingly participating in marketing through membership-based affinity groups through which, for example, buyers can receive airline frequent flyer miles when purchasing a home through the company.

"It's all about serving the client, adding value, and creating a level of comfort," says Joyce. "We want to be able to recommend people we feel offer the same level of quality that we do."

Bradfield Properties in 1990 introduced a real estate magazine, *Homes For Sale*, which continues to be sought-after today. In 1992, the

BRADFIELD PROPERTIES REALTORS HAS SEVEN RESIDENTIAL OFFICES IN SAN ANTONIO, AND CAN BE FOUND ON THE INTERNET AT WWW.BRADFIELDPROPERTIES.COM.

JOYCE AND BOYD BRADFIELD, WHO FOUNDED BRADFIELD PROPERTIES IN 1982, WITH THEIR GRANDCHILDREN (FROM LEFT) ALI, MICHELLE, KELLY, KAYLA, AND JORDAN

firm initiated the *Sunday Morning Home Show* on KENS-TV, a live-action video program that offers previews of local homes. Fully equipped to produce the television show at its corporate office, Bradfield Properties will soon have these videotapes on its Web site, making them available for corporate employees relocating to San Antonio.

Bradfield Properties prepares special-edition tapes, which are large groupings of homes in a similar price range. These tapes are made available for its agents listing presentations or for corporate employees relocating to San Antonio.

A complete relocation division works with corporations such as SBC Corp., Ultramar Diamond Shamrock, CENDANT Mobility Services, Associates Relocation, and Americorp Relocation to help those who are moving to or from the San Antonio area. Bradfield offers area overviews and tours to acclimate those transferring to San Antonio. An important part of its Web site, the relocation section allows users to compare cost-of-living factors with other cities across the country and collect information about schools, neighborhoods, cultural and sporting events, and the economy.

"It's part of an education process," says Petlin. "We show people the important areas of the city and help them compare prices on housing." The Internet address, videotapes, and other technology-intensive services indeed serve to educate the consumer, but ultimately, says Petlin, the company's Realtors make the difference.

A Dedicated Staff

New agents undergo extensive classroom training sessions, and all representatives participate in ongoing seminars to maintain a level of service excellence. Many agents are lifelong friends and associates of the Bradfields'. "The agents who are successful are out for the good of the client," says Petlin. "Our owners are involved and care about the agents, who in turn offer the same kind of personal attention and interest to their clients."

Despite being spread among many offices, the agents remain a close-knit group. Bradfield Properties holds annual awards ceremonies to recognize top-producing Realtors, and gives quarterly awards for outstanding sales and service. Individual offices recognize their agents' performance monthly, and everyone looks forward to companywide birthday celebrations and the annual picnic.

At its annual picnic, Bradfield Properties holds a silent auction to benefit a local charity. Employees support the annual United Way campaign, and many participate as board members and officers in the San Antonio Board of Realtors and local chambers of commerce.

Growth is definitely in the future at Bradfield Properties. A new office was opened in New Braunfels at the end of 1997. The Stone Oak office expanded into its own, 11,000-square-foot building. Also, the office on IH-10 West will expand into a larger space later this year. "We are still looking at the possibility of opening up more offices, if the timing is right and we feel we could start it with the right Realtors," says Joyce.

Bradfield Properties has the people, the expertise, and the resources to make any moving experience a satisfying one. That's why it's number one in the San Antonio area.

THIS HOME LOCATED IN A PRESTIGIOUS NEIGHBORHOOD WAS ONE OF THOUSANDS SOLD IN 1997 BY A BRADFIELD PROPERTIES AGENT.

THIS CUSTOM-BUILT HOME BY JAY W. BRADFIELD, BUILDER, INC. IS LOCATED IN ONE OF SAN ANTONIO'S NEW SUBDIVISIONS.

Bay Networks

BAY NETWORKS HAS ONE SIMPLE PURPOSE: TO REVOLUTIONIZE the way people work, learn, and play by eliminating the constraints of time and distance. To achieve that goal, the company offers a single source of open standards-based technology, service, and support that fulfills high-performance availability and interoperability networking requirements at all levels—from enterprise and service provider backbone environments to branch offices and remote users.

Bay Networks' San Antonio Internet/Intranet Customer Premise Equipment Division got its start in 1985 as Performance Technology, an industry leader in the development of award-winning, innovative local-area-network-based products for companies of all sizes.

Performance Technology's development staff was spearheaded by a group of San Antonio engineers who invented local area networking (LAN) while at the Datapoint Corp. during the 1970s. The group included John Murphy, inventor of ARCNET, the world's first commercial LAN, and Jonathan Schmidt, vice president of the research group that oversaw developments ranging from 8008 processor architecture (given to INTEL in 1970) to ARCNET and the advanced LAN technologies of the 1980s.

Performance Technology was purchased by Bay Networks in March 1996, and the small, local business with only 40 employees suddenly joined an international network of 6,000 employees with annual revenues in excess of $2 billion. But, although the company has indeed influenced the high-technology market internationally, it maintains its strong ties to San Antonio. Employees are active in the community, supporting local National Public Radio and PBS stations, and volunteering their time each year for the March of Dimes WalkAmerica.

Changing with the Times

Originally, Performance Technology manufactured enhancement products for the Datapoint DOS and RMS environments, including a file server, automated backup systems, and other utilities. Using that technology, the company created PC-based solutions including POWERLan, an award-winning LAN software; POWERsave, a tape backup and restore software; and POWERfusion, PC-to-UNIX software.

Acknowledging the increasing movement toward the Internet, in 1993, Performance Technology began developing Instant Internet, a complete hardware/software solution designed to connect an entire LAN to the Internet through a single Internet provider address. Introduced to the market in 1995, Instant Internet remains one of the world's best turnkey solutions that connect LANs to the Internet.

From September 1996 through October 1997, Bay Networks received a number of industry awards for Instant Internet, including *PC Computing* magazine's four-star rating and MVP finalist, *PC Magazine*'s Editor's Choice award and Best Product of the Year, and *Network Computing*'s Editor's Choice, Well-Connected Product of the Year Award, and Editor Refuses to Give It Back citations.

As the Internet becomes increasingly important, Bay Networks will continue to develop products that make it easier for companies and individuals to use the Internet. "Our goal is to provide a product that consistently delivers more high-level service to our customers, while reducing the complexity on their networks," says Paul Finke, vice president of the San Antonio division.

Indeed, Bay Networks takes the complexity out of network evolution by providing high-performance, highly available, easily managed networks that keep companies competitive in these fast-changing technological times.

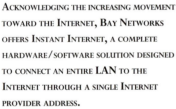

ALTHOUGH BAY NETWORKS HAS INFLUENCED THE HIGH-TECHNOLOGY MARKET INTERNATIONALLY, THE COMPANY MAINTAINS STRONG TIES TO SAN ANTONIO.

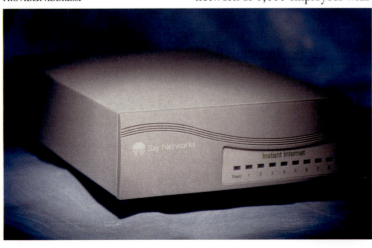

ACKNOWLEDGING THE INCREASING MOVEMENT TOWARD THE INTERNET, BAY NETWORKS OFFERS INSTANT INTERNET, A COMPLETE HARDWARE/SOFTWARE SOLUTION DESIGNED TO CONNECT AN ENTIRE LAN TO THE INTERNET THROUGH A SINGLE INTERNET PROVIDER ADDRESS.

COLDWELL BANKER D'ANN HARPER, REALTORS

D'ANN HARPER STARTED HER REAL ESTATE BUSINESS IN HER living room in 1986. Five months later, the six agents of D'Ann Harper, REALTORS moved into a 2,000-square-foot office; within two years, the company had grown to 18 agents. Then, in 1990, Harper purchased two Coldwell Banker company-owned offices. The number of agents went from 18 to 100 overnight.

Known today as Coldwell Banker D'Ann Harper, REALTORS, the firm serves San Antonio, New Braunfels, Canyon Lake, and the surrounding areas through its more than 200 sales associates and employees. The company includes multiple residential real estate offices, and divisions providing relocation and referral, property management and leasing, and apartment locator services. Harper also has the Coldwell Banker commercial franchise for San Antonio and the surrounding areas.

"Success has come through the work of good people, a good marketing concept, and a willingness to try new approaches," says Harper. "We have good, loyal people with common goals." Customer satisfaction is a primary element in the company's drive toward that goal. "It has to be a win-win situation for everybody," says Harper.

Coldwell Banker D'Ann Harper, REALTORS delivers results by having an Internet presence, a monthly magazine of listed homes, and a continuing commitment to technology. "We're trying to make it easier on our customers," Harper says. "We put ourselves in their shoes to see how new technology would be a benefit."

Harper's formula for success is succeeding: In 1994, Harper's peers honored her as the San Antonio Board of Realtors Broker of the Year. She has been a member of Coldwell Banker's Chairman's Circle, whose members are among the top 5 percent of all Coldwell Banker companies internationally, for eight consecutive years. Coldwell Banker D'Ann Harper, REALTORS ranks number two in residential real estate in the city, with sales of more than $307.7 million in 1997.

In 1996, the U.S. Directorate of Public Works awarded Coldwell Banker D'Ann Harper, REALTORS a two-year contract to offer real estate services at Fort Sam Houston for military personnel and Department of Defense employees. Harper also secured an area management broker contract from the Veterans Administration to handle its Bexar County properties through 2000.

Coupled with the firm's business success is a commitment to the communities where the company operates. Coldwell Banker is an international sponsor of Habitat for Humanity, and Harper's staff regularly volunteers to work on Habitat homes in the San Antonio area. The American Heart Association and Toys for Tots are beneficiaries of the company's annual fund-raising efforts. Harper also serves on the board of the Greater San Antonio Chamber of Commerce.

Steady growth, commitment to excellence, and dedicated customer service have positioned Coldwell Banker D'Ann Harper, REALTORS as a leader in San Antonio real estate, and the future holds more of the same. "We want to be number one," Harper says. "Not necessarily through the number of agents and offices we have, but through repeat business and quality of service."

"SUCCESS HAS COME THROUGH THE WORK OF GOOD PEOPLE, A GOOD MARKETING CONCEPT, AND A WILLINGNESS TO TRY NEW APPROACHES," SAYS D'ANN HARPER. "WE HAVE GOOD, LOYAL PEOPLE WITH COMMON GOALS."

MMI, Inc.

In the early 1980s, Robert Whitt IV was editor of the *Texican*, a Sunday supplement to the *Dallas Morning News* that covered events in the local Hispanic community. Dissatisfied with the poor quality of Spanish-language advertising in the supplement, Whitt was inspired to start his own agency to address the situation.

In 1985, Whitt founded MMI, Inc., a full-service Hispanic advertising agency, with one other employee. The company's billings that first year were $50,000. Within 10 years, the agency had grown to 12 full-time employees and billings that exceeded $10 million annually. The bulk of MMI's campaigns are targeted to the nearly 27 million people of Hispanic heritage in the United States, while the remainder promote the products and services of American companies to an ever widening market in Mexico.

GATT Paves the Way

Whitt can identify several factors that have made MMI such a success. For one, the United States had just signed the General Agreement on Tariffs and Trade (GATT) Treaty, which liberalized trade between the United States and Mexico. As trade barriers fell, Whitt recognized the opportunity to explore advertising and marketing south of the border. Secondly, Whitt saw an opportunity closer to home. Hispanics account for 10 percent of the total U.S. population, and are the fastest-growing minority in the country; however, Whitt realized that this portion of the population was being underserved by established advertising agencies. With the financial backing of three investors from his family, he selected San Antonio, then the fourth-largest Hispanic market and a gateway to Mexico, as the base of operations for MMI.

Whitt is now president and chief executive officer of MMI. Partner Eli Rodriguez directs the agency's creative side, and Ed Rutledge, also a partner in the business, oversees account service. Collectively, the team creates Hispanic marketing and advertising strategies for companies that are familiar names to English-speaking households, but perhaps not as well known to Hispanic families. MMI counts Time-Warner, Pace Foods, and Circle K among its clients who understand the value of addressing Spanish-speaking

MMI, Inc., a full-service Hispanic advertising agency, was founded in San Antonio in 1985.

members of the population in their own language.

"There's a certain segment of this population that requires a different type of communication, and in a socially relevant context," says Whitt. "Advertising to Hispanics on their terms is something that they can understand and feel good about. Many companies are beginning to see the importance of marketing and advertising to this segment of the population, and are utilizing firms such as MMI to reach them."

New Product Rollouts

MMI's secondary business is new product rollouts in Mexico, such as the sales and marketing campaign for Pace Foods to introduce Pace Picante Sauce in Mexico. MMI developed a business plan and identified potential distributors for the product, and even negotiated contracts between Pace and distributors. In another campaign, for the convenience store chain Circle K, the agency developed a franchising strategy prior to developing marketing and advertising.

"We go to work long before the media and advertising stage to identify sales potential for each business's market," says Whitt. He describes MMI's approach as pragmatic. "We base it on socio-economics to quantify the target demographic in order to help clients focus their approaches. We fine-tune what the overall piece of the pie is for them."

Although MMI has won numerous awards for its work, Whitt didn't realize the extent of the agency's success until a chance encounter opened his eyes. At a recent San Antonio conference on trade with Mexico, a speaker cited the 1991 introduction of Pace Foods into Mexico as a Harvard Business School case study. Whitt had no idea that his agency's work was being used as a model to teach others about how companies can introduce their products into Mexico, and it was a proud moment for the young company. "We're small, but very effective," he says.

The partners at MMI see only growth for the future. "Some people thought Hispanic advertising was a fad, but it's not," explains Whitt. "The level of professionalism has increased since we started in 1985, and consumers continue to reap the benefits."

MMI, too, has benefited from the growing market, but Whitt gives credit for the agency's success to the hard work of his employees. "Success has come from perseverance and good people," he says. "Having a thick skin and staying after your goal are the keys to any entrepreneurial business. You have to keep after it and take rejection with a smile every time."

THE BULK OF MMI'S CAMPAIGNS ARE TARGETED TO THE NEARLY 27 MILLION PEOPLE OF HISPANIC HERITAGE IN THE UNITED STATES, WHILE THE REMAINDER PROMOTE THE PRODUCTS AND SERVICES OF AMERICAN COMPANIES TO AN EVER WIDENING MARKET IN MEXICO.

Ultramar Diamond Shamrock Corporation

Created by the merger of Diamond Shamrock, Inc. and Ultramar Corporation in 1996, Ultramar Diamond Shamrock Corporation (UDS) is one of the largest independent petroleum and marketing companies in North America. A leading refiner, distributor, and retailer of petroleum products, the company also has about 6,400 branded retail outlets across 18 states and Canada, which provide customers with premium gasoline and oil products. With more than 23,000 employees, it is the sixth-largest convenience store chain in the United States.

Deep Roots in Texas

Headquartered in San Antonio since 1987, UDS' roots date to 1910, when a group of Pittsburgh manufacturers founded Diamond Alkali to produce soda ash, a major component in the production of glass. UDS' Texas history began nearly 20 years later, when John Sheerin founded Shamrock Oil and Gas Co. in Amarillo in 1929. Ten years later, in Sunray, Texas, Sheerin opened Shamrock's first service station.

Another Texas entrepreneur, Tom E. Turner, opened his first gasoline service station in 1943. Called Sigmor, the company incorporated in 1952; in 1960, Sigmor became a jobber for Shamrock Oil and Gas Co., distributing its products through stations across Texas. By 1983, Sigmor was one of the largest independent service station chains in the United States.

Diamond Alkali evolved into a major chemical company, and merged with Shamrock Oil and Gas in 1967. The new company, Diamond Shamrock Corp., established its headquarters in Dallas in 1978, and, in 1983, purchased Sigmor Corp. By acquiring Sigmor's retail marketing and refining assets, the Diamond Shamrock Refining and Marketing Company was created. In 1987, Diamond Shamrock Refining and Marketing spun off from its parent company, and became an independent, publicly traded Fortune 200 company in San Antonio.

The company's growth continued. In 1995, Diamond Shamrock Refining and Marketing bought 661 Stop N Go stores in Texas from National Convenience Stores, then the largest owner of convenience stores in the state. In 1996, when Diamond Shamrock merged with Greenwich, Connecticut-based Ultramar Corporation, revenues reached $10.2 billion, with assets of more than $4 billion.

UDS refineries in Texas, Canada, California, Oklahoma, Michigan, and Colorado have a combined production capacity of 650,000 barrels per day, and are expanding their petrochemical

Clockwise from top:
Shamrock Oil and Gas Co. was one of Ultramar Diamond Shamrock's (UDS) "ancestor" companies.

UDS stores offer patrons a wide variety of fresh and prepared foods and other convenience items.

UDS is building new Corner Stores, such as this one in Arizona, to serve customers.

production. The company's Mont Belvieu, Texas, facility has the world's largest underground natural gas liquids storage area, with 77 million barrels stored. An associated pipeline system allows UDS to provide a steady supply of products to its customers at competitive prices.

Becoming a National Leader

In 1997, UDS' acquisition of Total Oil of Denver added more than 6,000 employees to its roster and brought the total number of service stations to 6,400. Those stations market UDS brands, including Diamond Shamrock, Beacon, Ultramar, and Total, and sell more than 3.5 billion gallons of performance-tested gasoline each year in the United States.

"Ultramar Diamond Shamrock is changing from a major regional refining and marketing company to a major national refining and marketing firm," says Anne Cannon, public relations coordinator for UDS. "We're growing, and we're an increasingly bigger player in the convenience store, refining, and petrochemical markets."

UDS' convenience stores are customer-friendly, continually upgrading and adding services. "We are providing a service for our customers," says Cannon. "Convenience stores make it easier for people to get things done quickly in the limited time they have." The addition of major fast-food outlets; healthful, fresh deli foods; and gourmet coffees at its convenience stores, which also sell competitively priced gas, offers more services to the customer. This, in turn, translates to a good investment for shareholders.

Whether selling home heating oil, diesel fuel, petrochemicals, or gasoline at the pump, UDS emphasizes quality products at competitive prices. Committed to safety, the company strives to set an industry example of environmental initiative and compliance, practicing advanced technology in environmental protection.

THE ULTRAMAR DIAMOND SHAMROCK REFINERY IN ARDMORE, OKLAHOMA, PRODUCES ABOUT 68,000 BARRELS OF GASOLINE AND OTHER PRODUCTS EACH DAY.

Committed to San Antonio

UDS continues to invest in San Antonio, and is committed to supporting community efforts. In October 1997, the company moved its headquarters to a 225,000-square-foot, campus-style facility on the edge of Texas hill country. There, nearly 800 employees work in an open office environment with specially designed task lighting and ergonomic workstations. Even CEO Roger Hemminghaus' space is open and accessible. "With a sizable investment like this, it's a strong sign to the community that we are a permanent neighbor," says Cannon.

UDS is also a good neighbor. The company is a strong supporter of the University of Texas at San Antonio, and its corporate campus is adjacent to the university. Employees of UDS actively participate in United Way campaigns each year. In San Antonio, the company is responsible for donations of up to $800,000 annually, and its regional Shamrocks for Dystrophy program helps unite the community in contributing to the Muscular Dystrophy Association.

Today, UDS seeks additional acquisitions to maintain its top position in the refining and retailing industry. The company plans to continue expansion of fast-food outlets in its convenience stores to give busy families a one-stop opportunity for good food and inexpensive fuel. Ultramar Diamond Shamrock is poised to continue its growth into the 21st century, and is sure to be an important part of the San Antonio community for many years to come.

HEALTHSOUTH Rehabilitation Institute of San Antonio (RIOSA)

THE LARGEST FREESTANDING REHABILITATION CENTER IN San Antonio, HEALTHSOUTH Rehabilitation Institute of San Antonio (RIOSA) annually sees nearly 2,000 inpatients and more than 20,000 outpatients from throughout San Antonio, South Texas, and Mexico. The 108-bed hospital has more than 300 medical personnel on staff.

HEALTHSOUTH operates a full range of programs specifically designed to maximize the abilities of people suffering from a range of debilitating injuries and illnesses. Survivors of stroke, head and spinal cord injuries, orthopedic surgeries, respiratory disease, amputation, burns, heart disease, multiple sclerosis, Parkinson's disease, rheumatism, spasticity, chronic pain, and sleep disorders are all treated at this unique hospital.

HEALTHSOUTH, RIOSA's parent company, is the largest provider of rehabilitation services in the world, with more than 70 percent of the nation's rehabilitation beds, and is the largest health care provider geographically, with facilities in all 50 states.

HEALTHSOUTH's San Antonio network includes more than 18 centers that provide a variety of services, including ambulatory surgery, acute rehabilitation, physical therapy, specialized hand therapies, diagnostics, occupational medicine, therapy for sports injuries, and transitional living.

Making Patients Feel at Home

The average stay for patients at HEALTHSOUTH RIOSA is 19 days, and 30 percent of the patients are from outside the San Antonio area. Because of this, HEALTHSOUTH strives to make patients feel at home. But a homelike environment serves another purpose: It provides patients with a setting that allows them to relearn the real-life skills necessary to return to their own home.

Along with many specialized programs for specific problems, such as spinal cord injury or brain trauma, HEALTHSOUTH RIOSA offers a full complement of state-of-the-art treatment and rehabilitation equipment: weight and exercise machines, renal dialysis, an indoor aquatic-therapy pool, cardiac telemetry monitoring, ventilator services, pediatric services, and an outdoor mobility area.

And HEALTHSOUTH RIOSA has one feature that few other major rehabilitation centers are known to have: a therapeutic garden. With the help of a staff member who is a master horticulturist, patients enjoy fresh air, sunshine, and exercise as they grow flowers, vegetables, and herbs in raised beds. Patients can dry the herbs, which are used for seasoning, and use the flowers in arrangements.

HEALTHSOUTH RIOSA's special consideration for the families of its patients includes sponsorship of support groups. Families are one of the keys to rehabilitation, and HEALTHSOUTH makes every effort to provide for their needs during the patient's rehabilitation. This means not only support, but education and training. Staff at the facility have coauthored comprehensive guides for families, including *Living with Brain Injury: A Guide for Families* and *Living with Stroke*.

Making patients feel comfortable during one of the most difficult times of their lives is not an easy task, but HEALTHSOUTH RIOSA is committed to making patients feel at home. Such dedication ensures the hospital a strong place in the medical community for many years to come.

HEALTHSOUTH RIOSA OFFERS A FULL COMPLEMENT OF STATE-OF-THE-ART TREATMENT AND REHABILITATION EQUIPMENT, INCLUDING WEIGHT AND EXERCISE MACHINES, RENAL DIALYSIS, AND AN INDOOR AQUATIC-THERAPY POOL (LEFT).

HEALTHSOUTH PATIENTS ENJOY FRESH AIR, SUNSHINE, AND EXERCISE IN THE THERAPEUTIC GARDEN (RIGHT).

Phyllis Browning Company

San Antonio is a city with a rich cultural heritage, where living history can be found on just about every street corner. Yet it is a city constantly looking to the future, and there are always opportunities for creating new traditions. A brand-new tradition of quality, service, and excellence in San Antonio real estate was established in April 1989, when the Phyllis Browning Company opened its doors.

Founder and President Phyllis Browning started the company with just three associates and a goal to be, quite simply, the very best. Under the leadership of Browning and her partner, Mimi Weber, the company has grown to include more than 55 of the most successful and experienced real estate agents in the area, and with good reason: They love the city they call home and take pride in showing it to others.

New and innovative sales and marketing techniques, designed to create and maintain awareness of property trends, are constantly evolving at Phyllis Browning Company. Multilingual services are offered, and an entire department is dedicated to the relocation of newcomers to San Antonio.

Other services include commercial real estate, farm/ranch property, marketing, and sales. Phyllis Browning Company offers a comprehensive corporate relocation program, and was selected to help employees of Southwestern Bell, La Quinta, and HEB, among others, when their respective companies moved to new headquarters in San Antonio.

Phyllis Browning Company is committed to supporting the community as a member of the Greater San Antonio Chamber of Commerce, San Antonio Hispanic Chamber of Commerce, and Alamo Heights Chamber of Commerce. Phyllis Browning Company contributes time and resources to the San Antonio Economic Development Foundation, World Affairs Council, San Antonio public television station KLRN, San Antonio Witte Museum, Alamo Heights School Foundation, and Library Foundation. The company also supports numerous local children's charities through the Chrysanthemum Ball Association. Browning is currently a board member of the Greater San Antonio Chamber of Commerce and is a 1996 Recipient of the Small Business Award of the Year. Weber serves on the board of directors of San Antonio Botanical Center and JOVEN and is past president of the Charity Ball Association.

Phyllis Browning Company is the exclusive area affiliate of Christie's Great Estates, an international real estate brokerage network, and is a member of the Reliance Relocation Network. In a highly competitive industry, Phyllis Browning Company strives to be the very best and continues to lead the way, setting the standards for professionalism in San Antonio real estate.

Under the leadership of founder and President Phyllis Browning (left) and her partner, Mimi Weber, the company has grown to include more than 55 of the most successful and experienced real estate agents in the area.

Vencor Health Network–San Antonio

VENCOR IS THE NATION'S LARGEST FULL-SERVICE LONG-TERM health care company, spanning 46 states. Based in Louisville, Kentucky, this Fortune 500 company is considered a pioneer in long-term acute care and currently has 60 acute care hospitals, 311 skilled nursing centers, and 34 home health and infusion centers, as well as a variety of contracted ancillary services.

San Antonio is one of Vencor's largest market areas and is home to four of its health care facilities: Vencor Hospitals–San Antonio and South Texas; Normandy Terrace Nursing and Rehabilitation Center; and San Pedro Manor. Each of these facilities specializes in long-term care.

One Hospital: A Beginning

Vencor Hospital–San Antonio, which opened in 1988 as one of Vencor's first facilities, accepts acute care patients, ranging from children to the elderly, whose expected length of stay is more than 25 days.

"We provide care for those patients who are medically complex and chronically ill," says Ruth Lusk, executive director for Vencor Hospitals–San Antonio and South Texas. Nearly 150 physicians in all specialties belong to the staff of this full-service, 59-bed hospital, which includes a six-bed intensive care unit.

And Then There Were Four

Since Vencor Hospital–San Antonio's opening, admissions and average daily patient counts have climbed steadily. When physician demand called for a subacute care facility, Vencor Hospital–South Texas was born, and now maintains 49 beds. Both hospitals are accredited by the Joint Commission on the Accreditation of Healthcare Organizations.

In April 1997, Vencor purchased TheraTx, which owned Normandy Terrace and San Pedro Manor nursing facilities. Both facilities provide inpatient and outpatient rehabilitation therapies; pulmonary, hospice, and respite programs; and skilled nursing. Normandy Terrace also has a specialized Alzheimer's program, while San Pedro Manor offers an oncology/AIDS program.

A Complete Continuum of Care

With the recent acquisitions of two San Antonio nursing centers, Vencor now offers a complete continuum of care in that market, from intensive to long-term acute to skilled nursing and rehabilitative care. In addition, Vencor Home Health provides care for those needing attention after discharge from a facility.

"Vencor offers appropriate care for each degree of illness," says Lusk. "The objective is to move the patient from one level

VENCOR HOSPITAL–SAN ANTONIO, WHICH OPENED IN 1988 AS ONE OF VENCOR'S FIRST FACILITIES, ACCEPTS ACUTE CARE PATIENTS, RANGING FROM CHILDREN TO THE ELDERLY, WHOSE CASES ARE MEDICALLY COMPLEX.

SAN PEDRO MANOR NURSING FACILITY PROVIDES INPATIENT AND OUTPATIENT REHABILITATION THERAPIES; PULMONARY, HOSPICE, AND RESPITE PROGRAMS; SKILLED NURSING; AND AN ONCOLOGY/AIDS PROGRAM.

to another in the continuum based on their clinical needs." A critically ill patient may enter the system at Vencor Hospital–San Antonio; then, upon improvement, move to Vencor Hospital–South Texas; and later, move to one of the nursing facilities.

Vencor's nursing facilities emphasize rehabilitation and discharge to home. Nationwide, 62 percent of the nursing center admissions for rehabilitation return home. "We do an exceptional job, primarily with geriatric patients," says the administrator at San Pedro Manor. In most cases, nursing facilities' rehabilitation programs are designed to return patients to their homes.

Growth and Innovation

Vencor continues to look for opportunities to address the growing demand for its services. In late 1997, for example, the hospital announced plans to construct another long-term acute care facility on 2.3 acres of land near downtown San Antonio to provide service for that community. Founded on innovation, Vencor's plans are not so much in response to the current market, but in anticipation of developments within the medical community.

Vencor has long been an originator and developer of technology as it applies to patient care improvements. For example, Vencor currently uses a teleradiography

system that allows X rays to be transmitted electronically from 46 states to a central location for interpretation within minutes. A mobile version of the system is available for Vencor and other nursing facilities throughout the country. Paperless patient records follow patients as they move through the continuum of care, thanks to a touch-screen, records-access system known as VenTouch™.

Vencor's national network of hospitals and nursing facilities takes advantage of economies of scale to improve procedures and patient care. Additionally, an outcomes-based strategic quality plan links all facilities, so personnel may measure and compare results in long-term acute care, nursing home, and rehabilitation facilities. Vencor's mission is to provide the highest-quality health care in the most logical, lowest-cost setting.

Meeting the Needs of the Patient and the Community

In San Antonio, Vencor serves the community at large, as well as its individual patients. Volunteers from the facilities support charitable events around the city, and a sizable percent of management serves on local boards for such organizations as the American Lung Association, Hospital Welcome Lodge, and American Diabetes Association. The facilities also provide meeting space for health-related support groups and present health fairs.

As a result, Vencor Hospital's health network not only has the city's longest-running long-term acute care hospital, but it is the only full-service long-term health care provider. As the area's needs grow and change, Vencor will undoubtedly rise to the occasion.

CLOCKWISE FROM TOP LEFT:
RESIDENTS AT THE NURSING CENTERS PARTICIPATE IN OUTDOOR REHABILITATION ACTIVITIES.

ACTIVITIES COORDINATORS AT THE NURSING FACILITIES PROVIDE THE RESIDENTS WITH ENJOYABLE WAYS TO PASS THE TIME.

PAPERLESS PATIENT RECORDS FOLLOW PATIENTS AS THEY MOVE THROUGH THE CONTINUUM OF CARE, THANKS TO A TOUCH-SCREEN, RECORDS-ACCESS SYSTEM KNOWN AS VENTOUCH™.

Warm Springs Rehabilitation System

WHEN WORKERS DRILLING FOR OIL NEAR GONZALES, TEXAS, in 1909 struck a mineral-rich artesian well instead, no one dreamed it would become the foundation for a rehabilitation system that today serves nearly 2,000 inpatients and provides for more than 60,000 outpatient visits each year.

In 1937, Gonzales Warm Springs Foundation for Crippled Children was established as a 16-bed facility during the height of the polio epidemic sweeping the country. Polio patients came from across Texas and beyond to benefit from the therapeutic springs and the increasingly sophisticated health care services offered on-site. When the Salk vaccine ended the polio scourge in 1955, Warm Springs changed its focus to providing treatment for people with physical disabilities caused by catastrophic injuries and chronic disease.

Until the 1980s, Warm Springs was one of only three facilities in the state offering rehabilitation to victims of strokes, spinal cord and head injuries, and neurological and orthopedic problems. In 1989, Warm Springs underwent its first expansion by adding a rehabilitation hospital in San Antonio. The 65-bed facility was soon joined by four San Antonio outpatient facilities, and is now known as Warm Springs+Baptist Rehabilitation Hospital.

WARM SPRINGS+BAPTIST REHABILITATION HOSPITAL, LOCATED IN THE HEART OF THE SAN ANTONIO MEDICAL CENTER, HAS PROVIDED COMPREHENSIVE INPATIENT AND OUTPATIENT SERVICES SINCE 1989.

Meeting the Demand

The not-for-profit Warm Springs system relocated its headquarters to San Antonio in 1993 to meet physician demand for services. Today, the Warm Springs system operates three hospitals and 20 outpatient centers located across Texas. Its philosophy, however, hasn't changed since its founding: "To give personal, individualized treatment, helping every patient fulfill his or her potential to live as independently as possible."

A full-service, comprehensive rehabilitation system, Warm Springs offers acute inpatient rehabilitation as soon as patients are medically stabilized and can tolerate the recovery process, says Kay Peck, president and CEO, who adds, "Our goal is to help restore people to a functional lifestyle."

Orthopedic and pediatric patients, stroke and accident victims, and others who require intensive inpatient therapy undergo a full schedule of treatment. "We want to move patients to outpatient or home care as soon as possible, to bring them to the maximum level of independence," says Peck.

In 1993, Warm Springs augmented its services for catastrophic illness and acute rehabilitation to include noncatastrophic illnesses. That segment, which includes outpatient services for sports injuries and occupational medicine, is the fastest-growing area of patient service. Prevention-focused, it consults with, educates, and trains

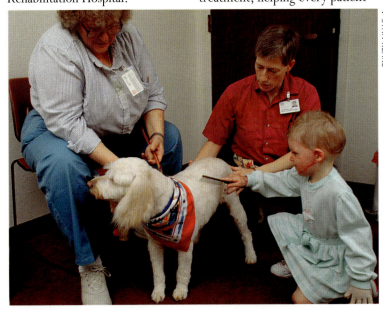

ANIMAL-ASSISTED THERAPY IS A SPECIAL PROGRAM AVAILABLE TO PATIENTS AT WARM SPRINGS HOSPITALS IN SAN ANTONIO AND GONZALES. IN SAN ANTONIO, THE PROGRAM FEATURES MAINLY DOGS AS THERAPEUTIC CATALYSTS FOR STIMULATING HEALING ACTIVITY. IN GONZALES, "HIPPOTHERAPY" (THE APPLICATION OF THERAPEUTIC HORSEBACK RIDING) IS USED, IN ADDITION TO PETS RANGING FROM BIRDS TO FISH.

participants to create environments that prevent conditions such as carpal tunnel syndrome and back pain. The division accounted for 35 percent of revenues within one year of its inception.

Focus on the Individual

Warm Springs' staff specializes in addressing the individual nature of each patient's needs, including age, family, and other factors. Rehabilitation services range from improving speech and motor skills to occupational therapy and daily living skills.

A leader and innovator in treatment and technology, Warm Springs is among the few to offer hyperbaric oxygen treatment in a rehabilitation setting. In this therapy, superrich oxygen is applied under pressure to increase the patient's oxygen absorption, with dramatic results. It can be useful therapy for those suffering from smoke inhalation or carbon monoxide poisoning, diabetes, or other cases in which wounds are slow to heal.

Adept at meeting patients' needs on their individual terms, Warm Springs provides access to the most modern titanium wheelchairs for sports participation, and also repairs steel and leather leg braces designed generations ago, yet still in use today.

In spring 1998, Warm Springs Rehabilitation System will open its first ResourCenter, which will promote an improved quality of life for an estimated 3,000 people with disabilities annually. The ResourCenter will provide support groups, vocational training, and more for children, adults, and seniors. Developed in collaboration with 40 other community agencies, it will also provide Internet videoconferencing services to allow users to connect with common entities throughout the state.

Community Outreach

Warm Springs impacts the San Antonio community through education programs such as Play It Safe, which instructs schoolchildren about prevention of spinal cord injuries, the importance of bicycle helmets, and diving safety. It also offers vocational training to assist employers in hiring and retaining people with disabilities. The foundation's annual fund-raising campaign, Warm Springs Round Table, solicits donations from the business community in return for information about occupational health concerns.

Wheelchair Sports is Warm Springs' most successful and visible community outreach program. Developed by the foundation in 1989, it began with limited sports opportunities. Today, the program offers nearly 500 participants a wide variety of recreational and competitive activities, including basketball, bowling, camping, canoeing, dancing, horseback riding, roller hockey, tennis, and waterskiing. Some Wheelchair Sports participants have competed at the International Paralympic Games.

In 1991, Warm Springs introduced ALLCANSKI, which encourages people with disabilities to waterski using specially adapted equipment. "We're introducing people with disabilities to things they'd never thought of doing," says Peck.

Warm Springs Rehabilitation System will continue to be an innovator in the changing health care environment. Warm Springs' driving force is to constantly keep its charitable mission in mind: to prevent and reduce disability by striving to assist others in maximizing their human potential. Says Peck, "Our focus continues to be, and will always be, individualized patient care."

▶ STAN KEARL

EVEN AFTER LOSING THE ABILITY TO SPEAK FOLLOWING A BRAIN INJURY, PATIENTS SUCH AS RUDY HERNANDEZ CAN MASTER NEW AVENUES OF COMMUNICATION THROUGH SPECIALIZED THERAPY PROVIDED BY EXPERIENCED WARM SPRINGS SPEECH PATHOLOGISTS SUCH AS CHAROLETTE UTZ (TOP).

ALLCANSKI, A TWO-DAY EVENT COHOSTED BY WARM SPRINGS WHEELCHAIR SPORTS AND SEA WORLD OF TEXAS, FEATURES EXPERT ADAPTED WATERSKIING INSTRUCTION BY TEXAS ADAPTIVE AQUATICS OF HOUSTON. THE EVENT, HELD FOR THE SIXTH TIME IN 1997, PROVIDES ACCESS TO THE EXCITING SPORT FOR MORE THAN 60 PEOPLE EACH YEAR (BOTTOM).

▶ JANELLE FISCHER

Sony Semiconductor Company of America

WHEN SONY ELECTRONICS INC. ACQUIRED ADVANCED MICRO Devices in 1990, it created Sony's first semiconductor manufacturing facility, as well as Sony's first semiconductor fabrication operation outside Japan. Since then, Sony Semiconductor Company of America has committed millions of dollars to improving the technology and products created at the San Antonio site.

Sony renovated the Advanced Micro Devices facility to accommodate increased production, and constructed a semiconductor wafer fabrication area that uses complementary metal oxide silicon (CMOS) technology. A new submicron technology facility produces commodity and high-value-added integrated circuit devices for communication, audiovisual, and computer applications. Sony Semiconductor Company of America also manufactures a wide range of products in its bipolar process technology lab. Products manufactured in San Antonio are shipped to destinations around the world.

Commitment to San Antonio

In 1994, Sony implemented a six-year, $260 million plan to expand and upgrade its CMOS fabrication unit and equipment to meet the burgeoning demand for higher-end computer chips. "We're always looking for new technologies and opportunities," says Barbara Ettipio, human resources director. Plans are currently under way for several products involving improved and new technologies.

In 1996, Sony Semiconductor Company of America was certified to the ISO 14001 standard, which develops guidelines for a fully functional environmental management system. It was the first Sony division, and one of only a few U.S. companies, to achieve that designation. "Sony is a very good example of a foreign-owned company that is very concerned about understanding the way things operate in the United States," says Ettipio.

Sony Semiconductor operates 24 hours a day, and many of Sony's current employees worked for Advanced Micro Devices and made the transition after the acquisition. "These long-term employees have been the key to the company's success," says Ettipio. "Even though we now employ more than 900 people, we still treat everyone with dignity, fairness, and respect."

In the competitive semiconductor industry, skilled employees are highly valued. Sony offers excellent benefits and a biannual environmental, education, health, and safety fair. The fair includes a variety of vendors on hand to answer questions about their products; free medical screening is offered; and educational institutions give information about programs during the two-day event.

Sony Semiconductor Company of America is also a community service leader in San Antonio. The company's Community Involvement Council donates equipment and funds to agencies and educational institutions, and, working in conjunction with the Alamo Community College District, Sony established a Semiconductor Technology Education Program at Northwest Vista College. This program provides continuing education for Sony employees, and prepares others for employment in high-tech fields. Sony employees also mentor students at Mary Hull Elementary.

With the increasing demand for sophisticated electronics, Sony Semiconductor Company of America is a major player in the production of communications, computing, and consumer electronics products. It is Sony's commitment to improved technology and manufacturing methods that will maintain the company's competitive edge well into the 21st century.

WITH THE INCREASING DEMAND FOR SOPHISTICATED ELECTRONICS, SONY SEMICONDUCTOR COMPANY OF AMERICA IS A MAJOR PLAYER IN THE PRODUCTION OF COMMUNICATIONS, COMPUTING, AND CONSUMER ELECTRONICS PRODUCTS. IT IS SONY'S COMMITMENT TO IMPROVED TECHNOLOGY AND MANUFACTURING METHODS THAT WILL MAINTAIN THE COMPANY'S COMPETITIVE EDGE WELL INTO THE 21ST CENTURY.

REGAN BRADSHAW

Euro-Alamo Management, Inc.

Euro-Alamo Management, Inc. was born out of its European investors' desire for a better, safer way to acquire commercial property and of its officers' ingenuity. Having already purchased the Alamo National Building and the Travis Building in 1992, and with plans to purchase the South Texas Building in 1993, the investors realized that they needed their own team of professionals to acquire, manage, and lease these and future properties. This team, they concluded, needed similar goals in order to avoid poor investment decisions.

In response to this need, Steve Stendebach, president, and Tony Russo, chief financial officer, formed Euro-Alamo Management in 1993. They chose San Antonio for its stable economic history, growth potential, and market size. Learning from the 1980s Texas real estate depression, Stendebach and Russo structured the company in a unique way.

Creating a New Concept

Recognizing that the fundamental flaw with most real estate investment advisers is that their profitability depends on transaction-based fees such as brokerage fees and leasing commission markups, Stendebach and Russo eliminated the fees entirely in exchange for bottom-line, property-performance-based incentive fees. In order to minimize expenses, operating costs of the company are distributed evenly over the portfolio. As properties are added, the costs decrease per property, further contributing to the bottom line.

Because Euro-Alamo Management charges no fees up front, it has no financial interest in acquiring properties that will not perform well. "We get paid on our results," says Stendebach. "That one significant difference fixed a lot of problems our investors had experienced with other management groups. This new concept is the key to our success and is our greatest accomplishment because it works beautifully."

Euro-Alamo Management today manages three historic office buildings in the heart of downtown San Antonio—the Alamo National, Travis, and South Texas buildings. The company also manages three modern buildings on the city's bustling North side—15600 San Pedro, Cherry Ridge Office Park, and Greatview Office Building. In total, the group has 650,000 square feet of commercial real estate under management. It also manages a 6,700-acre timber forest in upstate New York.

Even with these high-profile properties, the Euro-Alamo Management staff of 14 keeps a low profile in the city, because the firm's investors appreciate privacy. But this doesn't mean the investors are left in the dark; in fact, they receive half-inch-thick, monthly reports on each property, so they always know the status of their investments. "Because our investors demand accountability, they appreciate the effort we make to produce such detailed reports," says Stendebach. "And because we work exclusively for our investors, we are always available for consultation."

For the future, the company's staff will continue to focus on selecting properties that will perform well in order to attract new investors to its current group. And with the proven success of the company's unique concept for acquiring and managing properties, Euro-Alamo Management will be a vital part of the San Antonio community for many years to come.

From far left:
Euro-Alamo Management manages the Alamo National Building located in the heart of downtown.

The Greatview Office Building offers a commanding view of the San Antonio area.

Standing 10 stories tall, the South Texas Building was San Antonio's first skyscraper.

SBC Communications Inc.

BASED ON EQUITY MARKET VALUE, SBC COMMUNICATIONS INC. is among the five largest telecommunications companies in the United States, with 33 million access lines and more than 87 million potential customers nationwide. It serves the nation's two most populous states, California and Texas, as well as seven of the 10 largest U.S. metropolitan areas and 16 of the top 50. The company is poised to compete successfully in the $80 billion U.S. long-distance market, and its operations span six continents.

The scope of SBC Communications, whose income annually is more than $3 billion, is indeed vast, but its focus on the individual consumer never wavers. SBC refers to itself as "your friendly, neighborhood global communications company," which has promised, among other things, never to interrupt the family dinner hour with sales calls.

Edward E. Whitacre Jr. has been chairman and chief executive officer of SBC Communications since 1990. SBC established its corporate headquarters in San Antonio in 1993 in a move that brought 500 jobs from St. Louis to the Alamo City. By early 1998, continued growth and employee relocation had swelled the ranks of the company's San Antonio operation to approximately 6,700.

AN ENDLESS RANGE OF SERVICES

SBC's broad operations provide customers with an expansive range of services and products, from video and data telephone services, wireless communications, long distance, and Internet access to telecommunications equipment, voice mail, directory advertising, and cable television.

SBC offers products and services under some of the strongest brands in the industry: Southwestern Bell, Pacific Bell, Nevada Bell, and Cellular One. Southwestern Bell alone provides local telephone services to more than 15.7 million business and residential access lines in Arkansas, Missouri, Kansas, Oklahoma, and Texas. The company is committed to building value for shareholders, diversifying beyond local telephone services, and seeking opportunities to compete globally and in the U.S. long-distance market.

SBC pursues growth areas in the newly competitive U.S. telecommunications marketplace,

SBC'S APPLIED RESEARCH AND DEVELOPMENT ARM, SOUTHWESTERN BELL TECHNOLOGY RESOURCES, INC. (TRI), PROVIDES THE TECHNOLOGY LEADERSHIP AND EXPERTISE NECESSARY TO POSITION THE COMPANY AS A LEADING PROVIDER OF ADVANCED COMMUNICATIONS PRODUCTS AND SERVICES.

SBC'S BROAD OPERATIONS PROVIDE CUSTOMERS WITH AN EXPANSIVE RANGE OF SERVICES AND PRODUCTS, FROM VIDEO AND ADVANCED DATA COMMUNICATIONS, WIRELESS COMMUNICATIONS, LONG DISTANCE, AND INTERNET ACCESS TO TELECOMMUNICATIONS EQUIPMENT, VOICE MAIL, AND DIRECTORY ADVERTISING.

and has in place a disciplined strategy for growth. In April 1997, SBC completed its merger with Pacific Telesis Group, creating a company that today employs more than 116,000 workers, generates revenues of more than $23 billion, and earns income of more than $3 billion. Through its subsidiary, SBC International (SBCI), the corporation has jointly and wholly owned investments in telecommunications companies in Mexico, Chile, Switzerland, France, the United Kingdom, South Africa, South Korea, Israel, Australia, and Taiwan.

Since 1990, SBCI has invested nearly $1 billion in a consortium with France Telecom and Grupo Carso, in which SBCI acquired a minority interest in Teléfonos de México (Telmex), one of the world's fastest-growing telecommunications companies. With SBCI's assistance, Telmex access lines have increased more than 60 percent. In addition, more than 10,000 urban and rural areas have telephone service for the first time, long-distance usage has increased 44 percent annually, and cellular customers have increased from 35,000 to more than 713,000.

SBC continues to look for new ways to advance the telecommunications industry. Its applied research and development arm, Southwestern Bell Technology Resources, Inc. (TRI), provides the technology leadership and expertise necessary to position SBC as a leading provider of advanced communications products and services.

TRI focuses on wireless networks, which include Southwestern Bell's personal communications services infrastructure; voice technologies, such as voice-activated dialing; intelligent networks that use computers to offer customers "smart" telecommunications services; and information technology, which explores emerging Internet technologies.

Under Whitacre's leadership, the company has distinguished itself as an industry leader. In 1997, *Fortune* rated SBC the world's most admired telecommunications company in the first global reputation ranking published by the magazine. In 1998, SBC topped *Fortune*'s Most Admired Corporations list as the nation's number one telecommunications company for the third year in a row. SBC is also ranked among the top 30 Fortune 500 companies, with operating revenues of $25 billion.

Community Support

Although it is an international company, SBC is heavily involved in the communities in which its subsidiaries operate. The company supports social, economic, and civic development through donations of technology, scholarships and grant funding, employee volunteerism, and environmental awareness.

The SBC Foundation is at the heart of the company's outreach program. Each year, the foundation invests more than $20 million in scholarships, grants, economic development funds, and other deserving projects. Many of the scholarships that the foundation supports target students in technology-oriented academic tracks, such as engineering, math, and science. Scholarships also are available to minorities, at-risk students, and other special interest collegians.

Grants from the foundation also are invested in library improvements, civic development, and other projects among communities in its service territory. The foundation contributes more than $3 million each year to support the work of the United Way in helping people with special needs.

SBC Communications' service to the local community mirrors the corporation's focus on its individual customers; it's another way the company strives to be "your friendly, neighborhood global communications company."

BASED ON EQUITY MARKET VALUE, SBC COMMUNICATIONS IS AMONG THE FIVE LARGEST TELECOMMUNICATIONS COMPANIES IN THE UNITED STATES, WITH 33 MILLION ACCESS LINES AND MORE THAN 87 MILLION POTENTIAL CUSTOMERS NATIONWIDE (TOP).

SBC PRIDES ITSELF ON SERVING AS "YOUR FRIENDLY, NEIGHBORHOOD GLOBAL COMMUNICATIONS COMPANY" (BOTTOM).

PG&E Gas Transmission, Texas Corporation

On August 1, 1997, PG&E Corporation, a San Francisco-based marketer of energy services throughout North America and Australia, established an energy stronghold in Texas with the creation of PG&E Gas Transmission, Texas Corporation (PG&E GT-T). Formed from the merger of two entities—San Antonio-based Valero Energy Corporation's natural gas and natural gas liquids (NGLs) assets and businesses, and Teco Pipeline Co., a large, independent transporter of natural gas in Texas—PG&E Gas Transmission-Texas today operates more than 8,000 miles of natural gas pipelines, 500 miles of NGL pipelines, and nine gas processing plants.

The company is the largest subsidiary of PG&E Gas Transmission, the gas pipeline division of PG&E Corporation. PG&E Gas Transmission owns and operates pipelines in Texas and the Pacific Northwest. Sister companies include PG&E Energy Trading, which specializes in wholesale energy trading; PG&E Energy Services, which specializes in retail energy trading; and U.S. Generating Company, which participates in power generation and marketing nationwide.

Strong Texas Assets

PG&E Corporation, an energy powerhouse with assets of $30 billion, acquired Valero's natural gas and gas liquids assets, including processing plants and storage facilities, for $1.5 billion. By early 1998, PG&E GT-T, in combination with PG&E Energy Trading, had assets valued at $4.2 billion and average monthly revenues of $815 million.

More than 400 people are employed at the company's San Antonio headquarters and surrounding area, with more than 500 additional team members employed at pipeline and plant facilities across the state. PG&E GT-T supplies

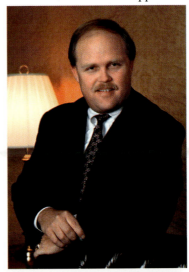

San Antonio residents, businesses, and utilities, among other clients, with natural gas for home, office, and power generation needs. Its pipeline capabilities and ample storage facilities allow the company to provide customers with reliable service even during peak demand times. The company also sells transportation services, allowing shippers to transport their gas through PG&E GT-T's pipelines.

PG&E GT-T is one of the most reliable transporters of natural gas in Texas, but its capabilities extend far beyond gas transportation and marketing. With a combined production of more than 100,000 barrels per day of NGLs from its nine state-of-the-art plants, it is among the nation's largest producers of natural gas liquids. It also operates three fractionation plants with a combined capacity of almost 100,000 barrels per day. These NGL products are ultimately used in the manufacture of plastics or in the heating and cooking sectors, or are consumed as a transportation fuel. The company is also the region's leading wholesale propane marketer. The NGL group markets to the major chemical companies, wholesale and retail propane distributors, refineries, gasoline blenders, and other chemical manufacturers.

Efforts to improve customer service, streamline operations, and operate plants more efficiently continue to pay off for PG&E GT-T. In early 1998, the company set an all-time NGL production record of 101,674 barrels per day. Plants processed 1.67 billion cubic feet of gas per day, up an average of more than 22 million cubic feet per day from the same period in 1997.

Terrence E. Ciliske, president and chief executive officer of **PG&E Gas Transmission, Texas Corporation**

In San Antonio, employees are active in an Adopt-A-School program whereby mentors work with students of Douglass Intermediate Learning Center.

Safety and Service Are Priorities

Although operational efficiency is important, safety is a major priority for PG&E GT-T. During 1997, as part of its continuing effort to promote safe practices, the company actively promoted two bills that passed the Texas General Legislative Session. The first bill requires developers of real estate to disclose the location of any pipelines or underground facilities to buyers of undeveloped lots. The second bill makes it a crime to intentionally remove, damage, or conceal a pipeline marker.

PG&E GT-T also strongly supported what is now known as the "one-call bill." This piece of legislation established a mandatory "call before you dig" program to prevent accidents and interruptions of service due to unintentional pipeline damage during excavation.

In October 1997, PG&E GT-T's operations department received the highest customer satisfaction ranking among all pipeline companies listed in an independent survey commissioned by the company. The survey measured the performance of the company in all aspects of service pertaining to customers' needs. Major technological initiatives in business information and operating systems enable PG&E GT-T and its sister companies to serve their clientele with increasing speed and

accuracy. Employees, however, remain the company's most valuable asset. In an ever-changing business, PG&E GT-T employees have a talent for seeking innovative ideas to enhance the company's services and provide the attention its customers deserve and expect.

The Competitive Edge

PG&E GT-T is also committed to the communities in which it operates. Volunteer councils in San Antonio, Houston, and other cities where the company has field offices participate in charitable endeavors, and the company strongly supports the United Way campaigns in these communities. As just one example of ongoing community support, the company has donated 60 computers to schools in rural Texas districts.

In San Antonio, employees are active in an Adopt-A-School program whereby mentors work with students of Douglass Intermediate Learning Center. In 1998, the San Antonio Area Mentorship Association presented PG&E GT-T and Valero, who participate in a joint mentorship program, with the 1997 Outstanding Mentorship Program Award. A PG&E GT-T employee was one of two San Antonio mentors to receive the Outstanding Mentor Award for starting positive relationships through mentoring.

With its dedication to safety and reliability, PG&E Gas Transmission-Texas has firmly established itself as a leader in the natural gas industry. Its commitment to consistent customer satisfaction and increased technological advances ensures the company's continued success.

PG&E GAS TRANSMISSION-TEXAS TODAY OPERATES MORE THAN 8,000 MILES OF NATURAL GAS PIPELINES, 500 MILES OF NATURAL GAS LIQUIDS PIPELINES, AND NINE GAS PROCESSING PLANTS.

Photographers

JOHN DYER moved to the San Antonio area in 1967 and operates John Dyer Photography, which specializes in photographing people. A graduate of Trinity University, Dyer received a master's degree in art history from the University of Texas at Austin. His work has appeared in the *Communication Arts Photo Annual*, three volumes of *American Photography*, and the 1990 and 1994 editions of *Gradias Photo Annual*. Among the awards he has received are the Flash Creative Excellence Award, the Dallas Society of Visual Communications Award of Excellence, and the Self-Promotion Excellence Award.

CHARLENE FARIS, a native of Fleming County, Kentucky, is the owner and operator of Charlene Faris Photos. Focusing on travel, historic, and inspirational photography, Faris has won numerous awards, including several from the National League of American Pen Women art shows. She was a 1994 Pulitzer Prize nominee for wedding photos of Lyle Lovett and Julia Roberts, which have now been published in more than 20 nations. Faris also completed an art project for the Hoosier Salon with a grant from the Indiana Arts Commission and the National Endowment for the Arts. Faris' images have appeared in several Towery publications.

LEE FOSTER, a native of Minnesota, is a veteran travel writer and photographer who lives in Berkeley. His work has been published in a number of major travel magazines and newspapers, and he maintains a stock photo library that features more than 250 worldwide destinations and 200,000 images.

TOMMY HULTGREN studied photojournalism at North Texas State University and San Antonio College. A native of New Mexico, he is now a San Antonio-based photographer with an emphasis on photojournalism and location portraiture. His clients include SBC Communications Inc., USAA, Diamond Shamrock, and *Texas Monthly*. The winner of numerous awards, Hultgren enjoys photographing old churches, and his coverage of the 1992 Republican Convention ranks as one of his most interesting experiences.

BUD LEE studied at the Columbia University School of Fine Arts in New York and the National Academy of Fine Arts before moving to the Orlando area more than 20 years ago. A self-employed photojournalist, he was named *Life* magazine's News Photographer of the Year in 1967 and received the Military Photographer of the Year award in 1966. He has founded photographers workshops in Florida and Iowa. Lee's work can be seen in *Esquire, Life, Travel & Leisure, Rolling Stone*, the *Washington Post*, and the *New York Times*, as well as in Towery Publishing's *Treasures on Tampa Bay: Tampa, St. Petersburg, Clearwater; Orlando: The City Beautiful;* and *Jacksonville: Reflections of Excellence*.

SCOTT MARTIN is employed at River City Silver. A graduate of Evergreen State College in Olympia with a bachelor's degree in photography, he focuses on black-and-white, fine art photography.

TRACEY MAURER, a self-employed photographer, graduated from the University of Texas at Austin and attended the graduate program at the Brooks Institute of Photography before moving to the San Antonio area in 1991. Specializing in commercial advertising, editorial work, annual reports, and food and product photography, Maurer's work has appeared in *Parenting* and *Esquire* magazines. Her clients include Luby's Cafeterias, HEB, Ben E. Keith Co., and Taco Cabana.

BUD NIELSEN, a certified professional photographer and New York School of Photography graduate, is the proprietor of Tucson-based Images International studio. With a collection of more than 100,000 stock images, Nielsen offers pictures of geographical locations throughout the United States, Europe, Africa, the Far East, and Central and South America. Subjects range from nature and people to travel and tourism. His clients include a plethora of magazines, newspapers, calendar and card companies, travel industry businesses, book publishers, and advertising agencies. In addition to having a permanent gallery in Phoenix—the Finch Gallery—Nielsen is represented by stock agencies located in California, New Hampshire, New Jersey, Australia, Belgium, and Germany.

© SCOTT MARTIN

MARK ORGANEK, a commercial photographer, received his bachelor of fine arts from the Pratt Institute in Brooklyn in 1977. He has lived and worked in San Antonio since 1994, and previously worked as a photographer in Austin for 10 years. His clients include both national and local businesses.

CARL PURCELL, a graduate of Indiana University, is the past director of photography for the Peace Corps and a former employee of the Agency for International Development in the State Department. Residing in Alexandria, Virginia, he and his wife, Ann, work together as the Purcell Team. Travel writers and photographers, they have a collection of more than 670,000 captioned color slides representing 98 countries. Their photography is distributed worldwide through 12 leading picture agencies, including Corbis Corporation, Wieck Photo Database, and Picture Network International. The Purcells' work has appeared in *Life, U.S. News & World Report, Condé Nast Traveler, National Geographic,* and the *New York Times,* among other publications. The Purcell Team has produced more than 120 photo CDs containing electronic images.

DONOVAN REESE hails from Minnesota and moved to Dallas in 1967. A student of photojournalism at the University of North Texas, he specializes in corporate, travel, and stock photography. Reese has worked with Texas Tourism, GTE, RSR Manufacturing, Tandy Corporation, Lone Star Gas, American Airlines, and Apple Computers.

BOB SCHATZ, who lives and works in Nashville, specializes in corporate, advertising, and stock photography for such clients as DuPont, IBM, NationsBank, UNISYS, and Service Merchandise. The recipient of numerous Addy Awards, Schatz has had images published in numerous magazines, including *Travel & Leisure, Business Week, Fortune,* and *Time,* as well as in Towery Publishing's *Memphis: New Visions, New Horizons* and *Nashville: City of Note.*

CLEM SPALDING, proprietor of Clem Spalding Photography, lives in San Antonio with his wife and three children. He specializes in photographing people and places, and has a client roster that includes Humana, Santa Rosa Health Care, Creative Street, Exxon, and Mercedes-Benz. An award-winning photographer, Spalding has had images published in *Texas Monthly, National Geographic,* and *Business Week.*

MICHAEL TREUTER, a native of Detroit, moved to the San Antonio area in 1984. Focusing on commercial photography, he works at Edge of Light, a San Antonio-based studio.

MICHAEL VASQUEZ specializes in portraiture and artistic stock photography, with an emphasis on people. His clients include New York Telephone, Prudential Insurance, Eastman Kodak, Coldwell Banker, Pennzoil, and various public relations firms.

CARY WHITENTON, originally from Laredo, moved to the San Antonio area in 1982. A graduate of both the Brooks Institute of Photography and the University of Houston, he specializes in commercial photography. Whitenton has an interest in photographing people and food, and his clients include Dillard's, USAA, La Quinta, Psychological Corporation, Southwestern Bell, Farmland Foods, Pioneer Flour Mills, and Valero.

LIZ GARZA WILLIAMS, originally from San Antonio, worked in Dallas for two years photographing for Mary Kay Cosmetics, *Today's Dallas Women,* Pier 1 Imports, and JCPenney before returning to the San Antonio area. With a focus on fashion, catalog, advertising, and editorial photography, she has worked for Hampton Brown Publishing; *Escante,* a lingerie catalog; and the United Way. Other projects include Hispanic advertising for Texaco billboards for KJS marketing, weekly newspaper inserts for *Images Magazine,* and head shots and portfolios for various talent and modeling agencies. Williams also enjoys scuba diving, traveling, and cooking.

OSCAR WILLIAMS has been in the photography business since 1977. His expertise encompasses advertising illustration, illustrative portraits, executive portraiture, and people illustration. He works with local and national companies, including Kinetic Concepts, Westinghouse, Southwestern Bell, and many medical institutions. Williams has also worked for a variety of advertising firms, such as Atkins & Associates, Anderson Advertising, Sosa & Associates, Eickhoff Hannan Rue, and Inventiva. He has received numerous awards presented by the San Antonio Advertising Federation, the New York Art Directors Club, the International Association of Business Communicators, and the Communications Arts Society of San Antonio. A former part-time faculty member at his alma mater, Trinity University, Williams is a founding member of the Communications Arts Society of San Antonio as well as of the Austin/San Antonio Chapter of the American Society of Magazine Photographers.

© SCOTT MARTIN

Other photographers and organizations that contributed to *San Antonio: A Cultural Tapestry* are D. Clarke Evans, Hillstrom Stock Photo, and the Institute of Texan Cultures.

Index of Profiles

Alamo Community College District 143
Bank One San Antonio 142
Baptist Health System 150
Bay Networks 186
Bradfield Properties Realtors 184
Catholic Life Insurance 148
City Public Service 162
Coldwell Banker D'Ann Harper, REALTORS 187
Crowne Plaza St. Anthony Hotel 154
Datapoint Corporation 177
The Dee Howard Co. 164
The Domestic Agency 182
Euro-Alamo Management, Inc. 199
Frontier Enterprises 166
GPM Life Insurance Company 158
The Greater San Antonio Chamber of Commerce 144
HEALTHSOUTH Rehabilitation Institute of San Antonio (RIOSA) 192
Kinetic Concepts, Inc. 178
Marshall Clegg Associates, Inc. 146
McCombs Enterprises 168
MMI, Inc. 188
Pape-Dawson Engineers, Inc. 174
PG&E Gas Transmission, Texas Corporation 202
Phyllis Browning Company 193
St. Mary's University 140
San Antonio Express-News 141
San Antonio Federal Credit Union 160
SBC Communications Inc. 200
Sony Semiconductor Company of America 198
Southwest Business Corporation 180
Southwest Neon Signs, Inc. 159
Ultramar Diamond Shamrock Corporation 190
United Services Automobile Association 156
University of Texas Health Science Center at San Antonio 170
Valero Energy Corporation 183
Vencor Hospital-San Antonio 194
Warm Springs Rehabilitation System 196
Waterman Broadcasting Corporation of Texas 176